Matt Pelton

COOKING UNDER PRESSURE

Delicious DUTCH OVEN RECIPES Adapted
FOR YOUR INSTANT POT®

OVER 80 RECIPES

Instant Pot® and associated logos are owned by Double Insight Inc. Used under license.

ISBN 13: 978-1-4621-2188-5

Published by Front Table Books, an imprint of Cedar Fort, Inc.
2373 W. 700 S., Springville, UT 84663
Distributed by Cedar Fort, Inc., www.cedarfort.com

Library of Congress Cataloging-in-Publication Data

Names: Pelton, Matt, 1976- author.
Title: Cooking under pressure / Matt Pelton.
Description: Springville, Utah : Hobble Creek Press, an imprint of Cedar
 Fort, Inc., [2017] | Includes index.
Identifiers: LCCN 2017057340 (print) | LCCN 2017060656 (ebook) | ISBN
 9781462128839 (epub, pdf, mobi) | ISBN 9781462121885 (perfect bound : alk.
 paper)
Subjects: LCSH: Pressure cooking.
Classification: LCC TX840.P7 (ebook) | LCC TX840.P7 P424 2017 (print) | DDC
 641.5/87--dc23
LC record available at https://lccn.loc.gov/2017057340

Cover and page design by M. Shaun McMurdie
Cover design © 2018 Cedar Fort, Inc.
Edited by Melissa J. Caldwell

Printed in the United States of America

10 9 8 7 6 5 4 3 2 1

Printed on acid-free paper

Matt Pelton

COOKING UNDER PRESSURE

Delicious DUTCH OVEN RECIPES Adapted
FOR YOUR INSTANT POT®

OVER
80
RECIPES

Front Table Books | An imprint of Cedar Fort, Inc. | Springville, Utah

Also by Matt Pelton

From Mountaintop to Tabletop:
A Complete Guide to Cooking Wild Game

The Cast Iron Chef

The Cast Iron Gourmet

Dutch Oven Pies: Sweet & Savory

Up in Smoke:
A Complete Guide to Cooking with Smoke

Beginner's Dutch Oven Cookbook

Dedication

I dedicate this book to all of my friends who stepped up when the pressure was tight (pun intended) to help me test the recipes for this book. I can't begin to tell you all how much that meant to me. Thank you all for all of your friendship and support over the years!

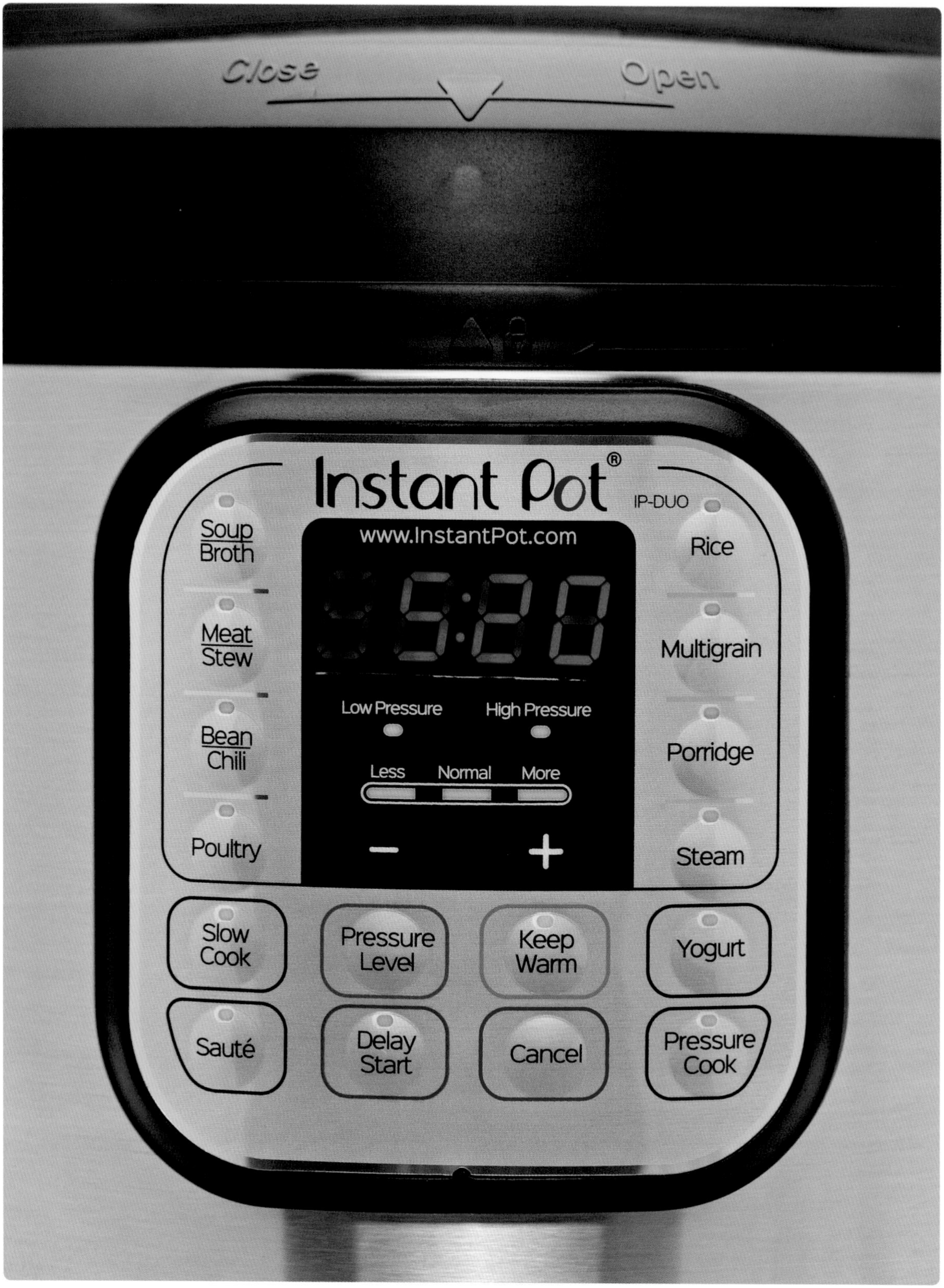
Close
Open
Instant Pot®
IP-DUO
www.InstantPot.com
5:20
Soup Broth
Meat Stew
Bean Chili
Poultry
Rice
Multigrain
Porridge
Steam
Low Pressure
High Pressure
Less
Normal
More
–
+
Slow Cook
Pressure Level
Keep Warm
Yogurt
Sauté
Delay Start
Cancel
Pressure Cook

Contents

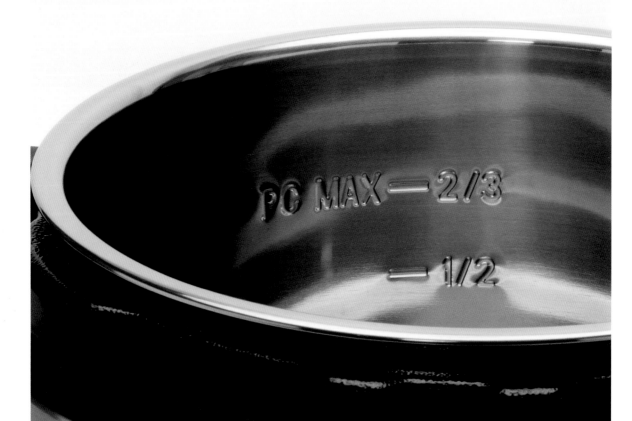

PC MAX — 2/3

— 1/2

Instant Pot® Duo Plus

Soup
Broth

Rice

Meat
Stew

05:30

Introduction

I have to admit that when I was approached about doing an Instant Pot® cookbook, I didn't know too much about the Instant Pot®. I had seen them and even eaten several meals made in them. I was familiar with pressure cookers. I've been cooking with stovetop models for my entire life. It has always been my go to when I needed to braise meat quickly or cook potatoes in a hurry. The very first time I used the Instant Pot®, I was hooked. This tool is super user friendly, easy to use, and very consistent. The instructions for setup were easy plug and play. I had my first meal cooked (chile verde) within two hours of opening the box. In all of my recipes following, I have included the instructions that I used to create the dish. There will be adjustments depending on the particular ingredients you use (some veggies and meats will have a higher moisture content than others). These recipes will give you a really good basis to have gourmet success with your Instant Pot®. A lot of the recipes that I have included in this book are award-winning dutch oven recipes that I have adapted to cook under pressure. Many of these recipes I have held back for a number of years and have released just for this book. Enjoy!

In this section I have compiled a list of cooking terms and tips that will help you in your quest to be a gourmet cook.

What Is an Instant Pot®?

The Instant Pot® is a brand name of electronically controlled pressure cookers. There have been many of these pop up on the market recently. A pressure cooker is a vessel that cooks food quickly by increasing the heat by increasing the pressure. For more than a century, pressure cookers have been used as a means to cook things quickly and have been critical in canning and bottling meat especially (the higher heat and pressure is needed to kill off harmful bacteria in meat). The Instant Pot® and others like it are fully functional pressure cookers but are very easy to use with their functions and controls.

Bases and Mother Sauces

ROUX: Roux is a mixture of fat and flour used for thickening liquids and for flavor. I use butter almost exclusively in my roux because of the flavor. There are several stages of roux. First is a blonde roux—this will have the most thickening power but will lend the least amount of flavor. You want to use a blonde roux whenever you make white or light color sauces. To accomplish this, you want to sauté the flour and butter together stirring constantly until the mixture smells like popcorn and will appear blonde in color. Next is the dark blonde roux—this roux is used for thickening darker sauces such as soups and stews and poultry gravy. It will not thicken to the point of the blonde roux but it will add loads more flavor and give you a lighter consistency. To achieve this, continue stirring and cooking past the blonde roux stage until the color appears similar to dark blonde hair. You should smell a slight nutty flavor. Next is light brown roux—this is the roux you should use for brown sauces and gravies. I use this exclusively for dishes made with beef. It provides a nice bold flavor but does not thicken as well as the blonde roux. To achieve this, continue cooking and stirring past the blonde point until the roux is the color of chocolate milk; it will have a very nutty aroma. Next and final is the dark brown or "brick" roux. I only use this roux for Cajun cooking. It is a staple for Gumbo. It's used primarily as a flavor and not nearly as much for thickening. To achieve this, continue cooking past the light brown stage. Stir rapidly at this point or it may burn. The color will become a rich brownish red and will have a very strong smell. Be careful as it is easy to overcook the roux and burn it.

Regardless of the roux that you use, make sure to constantly stir it. When you mix in your liquid ingredients, it is better if they are cold. The cold liquid poured into a hot roux will create a chemical reaction with the starches and literally explode them into the sauce creating smaller bonds and therefore a smoother sauce. Your grandma's roux likely consisted of stirring in flour into the bottom of the skillet after cooking pork chops or chicken that were cooked in butter or oil. She then poured water and slat and whisked it into a gravy for the meal. This is still a great technique, especially to match the flavor profile. Now that you understand what a roux is, you can make a superior sauce using the same technique.

MIREPOIX: This is the base of so many recipes. It's very easy to make and provides the building blocks for wonderful flavors. It consists of 2 parts onion, 1 part carrots, and 1 part celery cooked in oil or butter to "sweat" the essences, and then liquid is added to make a sauce.

SAUCE TOMATE: This red sauce is the base for a lot of Italian and French dishes. The red sauce is rich, bold in flavor, and will add a depth to all of your red sauce dishes. It consists of onions, carrots, celery, tomatoes, bacon grease, parsley, and black pepper. It is cooked for several hours traditionally but with the Instant Pot®, it is much quicker.

BECHAEMEL: This is also known as white sauce. It is a milk and cream based sauce that is the base for many soups, stews, and sauces. It is made by making a blonde roux and adding milk, cream, and spices until it is thickened.

VELOUTE: This sauce literally translates to velvet from French. It is a light sauce made from chicken, turkey, fish, or vegetable stock mixed with a roux. It makes very elegant gravies and sauces.

ESPAGNOLE: This classic brown sauce is the base of so many dishes and sauces from classic beef stew to gravy to demi-glace. It consists of browned mirepoix, light brown roux, tomato puree, and beef or lamb stock. I use this sauce in dishes such as beef bourguignon.

HOLLANDAISE: This sauce is a fat suspension sauce made from egg yolks, lemon juice, salt, and butter. It is extremely elegant and flavorful. It is perhaps best known for being the sauce poured over eggs benedict, though most of the commercial versions of this dish use sauce from a package that can't come close to comparing to the real thing.

Potatoes

Everyone just assumes that a potato is a potato but there is a lot of difference between varieties and what they are used for. Starchy potatoes are used for baked potatoes and whipped potatoes where a light fluffy texture is desired. They don't do well in soups and salads as they fall apart and create a grainy texture. All purpose potatoes are the best for use in mashed potatoes. Waxy potatoes are best used for potato salads, soups, and stews; they hold together much better but have too sticky of a texture for mashed or baked.

STARCHY POTATOES: Russets

ALL PURPOSE: Yellow, Yukon Gold, White, and Large Red

WAXY: Baby Red, Baby White, French Fingers, Purple, Small Yellow, New Potatoes

Onions

There is a world of difference in onions and their various uses. Some are best raw and taste terrible cooked. Some (sweet) are best cooked. Others have a mild sweet flavor and others a spicy sharp flavor. In all of the cooking seminars I do, onions are the least understood. As a rule of thumb, if the onion is taller than it is wide, it is going to be sharp for the variety. If it is wider than it is tall it will be sweet for the variety. I will list the onions in three categories: raw, sweet, and all purpose. Another rule of thumb for cooking onions is the size of the dice matters. If you want more of a sharp onion flavor, dice it small. If you want a milder sweet onion flavor slice it large or keep it whole. I will have instructions for dicing in every recipe that calls for them. You can adjust this as you wish–I just listed it the way I diced them.

RAW: Purple, Bermuda, and White onions, best as garnish, salads, sandwiches, or for salsas or similar

ALL PURPOSE: Yellow onions, Shallots

SWEET: Walla Walla, Sweet, New Mexico Sweet, Sweet Yellow, Spring onions

Beans

When cooking beans there are some techniques that will save you from bean's reputation on our digestive system. If you are cooking beans from dried, soak them for several hours to overnight in water, salt, and a small amount of baking soda. Be sure to remove any bad beans after the soaking process. You can then cook them in liquid without too many problems. This soaking allows the natural enzymes in the beans to be activated and break down some of the proteins that cause the gas. It also makes them easier to digest. With canned beans you don't have the same problem if you rinse and drain them from the can.

Salt

I will only use sea salt in any of my recipes. There is a huge difference in salts and the amounts you should use. Sea salt is the healthiest option and has a milder and sweeter flavor. Table salt is the strongest and least healthy option. If you use table salt, you will need to reduce the amount specified in my recipes. Kosher salt is not called kosher because it was blessed by a rabbi, it is called kosher because it is designed to remove the blood from the meat. It is really good for use in curing meat as well.

Cooking Techniques and Definitions

SAUTÉ: to cook in oil or butter. Many of my recipes use sauté as part of the recipe.

ROAST: To cook without touching the liquid or the bottom of the pan. This is used for most full cuts of meat. It keeps all of the flavor and nutrition in the meat, providing only drippings for the sauce, if any.

BRAISE: To cook in liquid—a lot of the recipes in this book use braising; it works well for the tool. One trick of braising is not to completely submerge the meat with sauce or liquid.

SEAR: Searing is sautéing meat in extremely hot oil in order to create a crust for flavor, appearance, and moisture retention. It is important to allow meat to relax after searing as the edge reaches temperatures of over 500 degrees to sear properly. If you don't relax the meat, the outer layer of the meat will turn out very dry before the middle is cooked through.

REVERSE SEAR: This is exactly what it sounds like. You cook the meat first, generally roasting, and you finish it off by searing it in hot oil. This is a very good technique to employ when using the Instant Pot® as the pressure will oftentimes soften the sear. Again, let the meat relax a little bit after cooking before reverse searing.

DIGITAL THERMOMETERS: I can't stress enough how important it is to have a good instant read instant thermometer. The very best available are made by thermoworks out of Utah, but there are many available on Amazon for purchase. The old type thermometers are too slow and often times not accurate as they get older. Having a good thermometer will make the difference between perfectly cooked meat or raw or overcooked meat. Here are some temperatures you should use:

BEEF: *Rare* 125–130 degrees | *Mid-Rare* 135 degrees | *Medium* 140 degrees | *Medium-Well* 145 degrees | *Well Done* 150 degrees | *Shredded* or *Braised* 200 degrees.

POULTRY: *Breasts* 165 degrees | *Thighs* and *Legs* 180 degrees. 165 is safe but will still look pink near the bone.

PORK: 145 degrees, it will still be slightly pink | 155 degrees if you want it cooked through | *Braised* or *Pulled* 200 degrees.

SEAFOOD: 125 degrees.

GROUND RED MEAT OR PORK: 155 degrees.

GROUND POULTRY: 165 degrees.

WILD GAME: 125–140 degrees. Do not exceed these temps as it will dry out with very little fat in the meat.

POULTRY GRAVY | PAGE 4

SAUCE TOMATE | PAGE 9

BÉCHAMEL | PAGE 6

CHAPTER 1:
Basic Recipes and Mother Sauces

This chapter has some basic recipes that will help you in building many other recipes within the book. The Mother Sauces are so called because they are staples in French cuisine used as the base of many of their recipes.

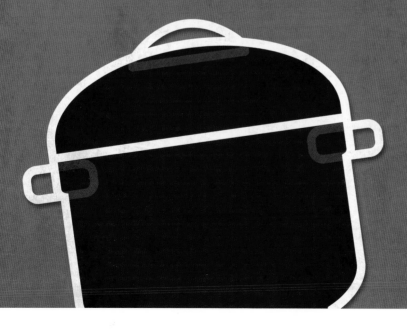

Espagnole or Brown Sauce

This sauce is so easy to make and is so essential in so many of the recipes here. It can also be used as a stand alone as a gravy for rice or potatoes. The sauce calls for flour, but cornstarch can be substituted just as easily.

4 Tbsp. real butter	3 cups beef stock
1 cup onions (¼ diced)	3 Tbsp. tomato puree
½ cup diced carrots	1 Tbsp. beef base
½ cup diced celery	Salt and pepper to taste
4 Tbsp. flour	

1. Set the Instant Pot® to Sauté high. Melt the butter in the bottom and brown the onions, carrots, and celery. Stir it well until it is browning.

2. Stir in the flour mixing well. Cook for several minutes whisking well until it smells like popcorn and starts to turn light brown.

3. Add the stock, tomato puree, and beef base. Stir it for a minute until is thickened.

4. Cook for several minutes. You can strain the veggies out for a smooth texture, puree it with an immersion blender, or keep the veggies as they are for stews.

Poultry Gravy

Whether you are using it for chicken or turkey, this basic sauce recipe always turns out great. I have had so many people tell me that it is the best gravy they've ever tasted. That's surprising because it is so simple to make.

4 Tbsp. real butter

4 Tbsp. flour

3 cups chicken stock

2 Tbsp. chicken or turkey base

(optional) Any drippings from the turkey or chicken you roasted

1. Begin by selecting sauté high on the Instant Pot®. Place the butter in the bottom and stir in the flour until it is well incorporated and it starts to smell like popcorn.

2. Stir in the chicken stock and the base and stir in well.

3. Place the lid on and cook manual pressure low for 5 minutes; let it bleed off naturally.

4. Whisk it well after taking the lid off and season with sea salt and pepper to taste.

Stock

Almost any great sauce starts with a great stock. This recipe works the same whether you are making beef stock, chicken stock, or vegetable stock. Once stock is made, it can be frozen and used at any time.

1 lb. of bones (beef, chicken, pork)—leftover rotisserie works well as well as things like oxtail, etc.

3-5 carrots kept whole, trimmed only enough to fit in the pot

2 onions kept whole, paper on

5 celery stalks, keep leaves

4 cloves garlic, with paper on

3 bay leaves

½ lb. mushrooms, any variety

½ lb. fresh parsley, kept whole

6 cups water

3 tsp. sea salt

1. Place all the ingredients into the Instant Pot®. Place the lid on and select meat/stew and set the time for 90 minutes.

2. Let the pot bleed off naturally and let it relax for at least 1 hour. Drain the stock through a sieve and remove all of the solids.

3. Let it cool down and refrigerate or freeze.

Béchamel

This white sauce is a mother sauce and is the basis of a lot of my recipes. It is a good one to learn.

4 Tbsp. real butter

4 Tbsp. flour

4 cups milk (whole milk is
preferred)

½ pint heavy cream

Salt and pepper to taste

1. Turn the Instant Pot® onto sauté. Place the butter in the bottom. Add the flour and whisk it in until the flour is well incorporated and starts to turn blonde and smell like popcorn.

2. Pour in the milk slowly and whisk it well.

3. Place the lid on and select manual pressure low for 5 minutes. Let it bleed off naturally. Whisk it very well and slowly fold in the cream.

4. Add the salt and pepper to taste. You can now use this base for making many soups and sauces.

Mornay Sauce

This white cheese sauce is the basis of a lot of my recipes. It is a good one to learn.

4 Tbsp. real butter

4 Tbsp. flour

4 cups milk (whole milk is preferred)

½ pint heavy cream

½ lb. American cheese, cut into cubes (like Velveeta or similar)

½ lb. shredded cheddar or mixed cheese like Mexican blend

Salt and pepper to taste

1. Turn the Instant Pot® onto sauté. Place the butter in the bottom. Add the flour and whisk it in until the flour is well incorporated and starts to turn blonde and smell like popcorn.

2. Pour in the milk slowly and whisk it well.

3. Place the lid on and select manual pressure low for 5 minutes. Let it bleed off naturally. Whisk it very well and slowly fold in the cream.

4. Add the cheese a little at a time and fold it in.

5. Add the salt and pepper to taste. You can now use this base for making many recipes.

Sauce Velouté

This Mother sauce is the base of many poultry or seafood dishes. It will add a richness to your dish. You can use this recipe for the most elegant gravy you've ever had for Thanksgiving—use the neck from the turkey to make it. It does take a little extra time and care but it's worth it.

FOR THE WHITE STOCK
Raw chicken, turkey, or seafood bones

1 large sweet onion kept whole

1 cup carrots sliced

1 cup celery sliced

¼ cup parsley

4 cups water

2 tsp. sea salt

2 tsp. coarse black pepper

FOR THE VELOUTÉ
4 Tbsp. real butter

4 Tbsp. flour

3 cups white stock

1. Begin by adding all of the white stock ingredients to the Instant Pot®. Place the lid on and select soup and set the time for 15 minutes. Let the pressure bleed off naturally and continue cooking on the warm setting for 1 hour before opening the lid.

2. Strain the liquid off with a sieve lined with cheesecloth. Set aside.

3. Melt the butter in the Instant Pot® on sauté and whisk in the flour creating a blonde roux.

4. When the roux is blonde in color and smells like popcorn, pour in the white stock a little at a time whisking it in. Cook it until it has thickened. You can now use this as a base for many recipes or as a gravy or sauce. Be sure to keep the Velouté warm until you are ready to use it.

Sauce Tomate

This Mother sauce is the base for a lot of the red sauces in this book, such as Swiss Steak or Marinara sauce. It is incredibly rich in flavor and will beat out anything you can make from a can.

1 lb. salt pork, pancetta, or bacon, diced

2 cups sweet onions, ¼-inch diced

1 cup carrots, diced

1 cup celery, diced

2 cloves garlic, minced

2 cups tomatoes, diced

3 bay leaves

¼ cup fresh parsley

2 tsp. sea salt

2 tsp. coarse ground black pepper

1 tsp. thyme or 1 sprig of fresh thyme

4 cups chicken stock

1. Begin by selecting sauté on the Instant Pot®. Brown the salt pork, pancetta, or bacon really well. Remove the meat, leaving the grease behind.

2. Add the onions, celery, and carrots to the grease, stir well, and cook until they are starting to brown.

3. Add the remaining ingredients, place the lid on the pot, and select soup and set the time for 20 minutes. Let the pressure bleed off naturally.

4. Remove the bay leaves and blend the remainder of the ingredients until smooth using an immersion blender. You can now use this base to make many other recipes.

Hollandaise Sauce

This Mother sauce is a staple for eggs benedict and the base for one of the recipes in this book. The Instant Pot® wasn't my first choice for making this, but the way it's designed with the trivet made it work easily.

6 egg yolks

3 tsp. fresh squeezed lemon juice

1 tsp. sea salt

2 sticks real butter

pinch of smoked sweet paprika

1 cup water

1. Mix the egg yolks, lemon juice, and salt together in a 7-inch metal or glass bowl that fits inside the Instant Pot®.

2. Pour the water in the bottom of the Instant Pot® and set the trivet in the bottom and select sauté high.

3. Melt the butter and set to the side.

4. When the water starts to boil, set the bowl inside the Instant Pot® and whisk the egg mixture well, adding the melted butter a little at a time and making sure it's well incorporated each time. Continue to do so until all of it is incorporated. You can discontinue when you get to the bottom of the butter where the milk fats have settled out.

5. Turn the Instant Pot® to warm and keep it in there until it is ready to use. Sprinkle the paprika in at the end.

THANKSGIVING TURKEY BREAST | PAGE 15

COLA SIRLOIN TIPS | PAGE 27

THE BEST MASHED POTATOES | PAGE 14

CHAPTER 2:
American Classic Recipes

These recipes are my take on some classic American recipes I have adapted to cook in a pressure cooker. Most of these I consider comfort food items that most people will enjoy.

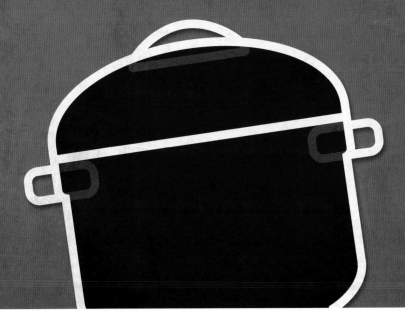

The Best Mashed Potatoes

I started making these mashed potatoes during my time as a professional chef. I used an old manual pressure cooker on the range top. I had a lot of compliments about them being the best potatoes people have ever had. For me, they were just really quick and easy to make. It is important to note that different varieties of potatoes are used for entirely different results. This is super important in this recipe for the texture to turn out right. Large russet potatoes, for example, are very starchy and will produce very light and fluffy mashed potatoes; they are best for baked potatoes. Small red potatoes have a higher sugar content and will produce heavy and sticky mashed potatoes; they are best used for soups and salads where they stay together well. This recipe calls for yellow potatoes—Yukon gold potatoes will work as well. They produce a mashed potato that is elegant, substantial, and flavorful. It is also super important not to peel these potatoes. The peel is where most of the vitamins are and for this to work properly it needs the peels intact to cook. If you don't like to eat the peels, remove them after the potatoes are cooked before mashing— they will come right off.

3-5 lbs. of yellow or gold potatoes, kept whole and washed well

3 cups water

1 Tbsp. sea salt

1 stick real butter

½ pint heavy cream

2 tsp. white pepper

1 tsp. black pepper

Sea salt to taste

1. Pour the water and salt into the Instant Pot® and place the potatoes whole arranging them as best as you can.

2. Place the lid on the Instant Pot® and set to manual pressure high and cook for 20 minutes. Let the pressure bleed off naturally.

3. Drain the liquid, add the remaining ingredients, and mash using a potato masher until it is a smooth consistency and mixed together well.

Thanksgiving Turkey Breast

I really enjoy the Turkey breast cooked in the Instant Pot®. It turns out incredibly moist and tender. The Instant Pot® is not big enough for a full turkey, but is okay for a turkey breast.

3-4 lbs. boneless turkey breast

4 Tbsp. canola oil

1 stick real butter

1 cup chicken stock

1 sprig fresh sage

2 sprigs fresh thyme

1 sprig fresh oregano

2 tsp. smoked sweet paprika

1 lemon, cut into slices

4 cloves garlic, peeled and kept whole

2 tsp. sea salt

2 tsp. coarse ground black pepper

1. Begin by trimming the breast to fit inside of the Instant Pot®. Heat up the oil in the bottom of the Instant Pot® by selecting sauté.

2. Brown the turkey breast well, remove from the Instant Pot®, and sprinkle the salt, pepper, and paprika on the breast.

3. Add the remaining ingredients to the Instant Pot® and scrape the bottom with a plastic or wooden scraper.

4. Place the trivet in the bottom and set the breast on the trivet. Close the lid and select meat/stew and set the time for 40 minutes. Let the pressure bleed off naturally.

5. Check the temperature and make sure it is at least 165 degrees in the center. If not add more time.

6. Let the breast relax for 10 minutes before slicing. Dredge the slices through the butter mix before serving.

Chicken and Rice

We had this dish a lot growing up. It still is one I look forward to.

2 lbs. bone-in skin-on chicken
    thighs

3 cups rice

3 cups water

1 packet Lipton onion soup mix

Sea salt and pepper for the chicken

Olive oil for browning the chicken

1. Trim the chicken thighs well, removing any excess skin and fat and making them all similar in size and shape.

2. Pour some olive oil in the bottom of the Instant Pot®. Turn it on to sauté and wait until the oil is hot. Brown the chicken well on both sides carefully lifting it off the bottom to make sure you don't tear the skin. Set the chicken aside.

3. Pour the rice, water, and soup packet in the pot and stir well, making sure to scrape the bottom with a wooden or plastic scraper. Place the chicken on top of the rice with the bone side down. Place the lid on the Instant Pot® and set to rice for 25 minutes. Let the pressure bleed off naturally.

4. Check the internal temperature of the thighs near the bone and make sure that it is at least 165 degrees. Stir butter into the rice and serve.

Chicken and New Potatoes

I came up with recipe on a hunting trip with my family. It is simple to make and it has become a staple of every hunting camp since.

4 Tbsp. real butter

4 Tbsp. flour

3 cups water

3 Tbsp. chicken base

2-3 lbs. chicken tenderloins or breasts cut into strips

3 (14-oz.) cans of whole new potatoes sliced in halves or quarters

Salt and pepper to taste

1. Turn the Instant Pot® onto sauté and high temperature. Place the butter in the bottom and stir it until it is melted. Whisk in the flour and stir it for several minutes until you can smell the flour cooking and it has turned blonde in color.

2. Slowly pour in the water and add the chicken base. Stir until thickened. Add the chicken tenders and stir them in until they are coated with the sauce.

3. Drain and slice the new potatoes and add them to the top of the chicken. Put the lid on the Instant Pot® and hit clear. Turn the Instant Pot® to Stew/Meat and high temperature.

4. Let the Instant Pot® run it's cycle and bleed off naturally. Remove the lid and stir it well. Add salt and pepper to taste and serve.

Lemon Zest Salmon

I never would have considered cooking salmon in a pressure cooker before I tried it. The result was a super moist poached type salmon that can be made in a hurry.

8 oz. salmon fillet

½ lemon, squeezed and zested

2 Tbsp. brown sugar

1 Tbsp. real butter

Sea salt and pepper to taste

½ cup water

1. Fold a piece of foil up that will fit in the Instant Pot®. Place the salmon fillet skin side down in the foil.

2. Add all of the ingredients except the water on top of the salmon fillet.

3. Pour the water in the Instant Pot® and hit the sauté button. Let the water boil and hit the clear button.

4. Place the foil with the salmon on the trivet and lower it into the pot. Close the lid and hit manual, pressure, high, and set the time for 5 minutes.

5. When the time is finished, release the pressure manually. Remove the foil, drizzle the juices back over the top, and serve.

Ninety-Minute Sunday Dinner

This is an American Classic. This dish would normally have to be started in the morning and take most of the day to cook. With the Instant Pot®, this takes only an hour for that gooey goodness of beef and carrots served over potatoes or rice.

3-5 lb. chuck roast

3 Tbsp. canola oil

¼ cup flour or 2 Tbsp. of corn starch

1 onion, left whole with ends removed

1 lb. baby carrots

Salt and pepper to taste

Single batch of Brown Sauce Recipe found on page 3

1 Tbsp. beef base

2 Tbsp. Worcestershire sauce

1. Set the Instant Pot® to sauté, select the high option. Add the oil to the bottom. Let it heat up for several minutes.

2. Salt and pepper the roast heavily on both sides. Brown the roast on both sides until well browned. Dust the roast with the flour and let it relax while you make a brown sauce.

3. Melt the butter (from the brown sauce recipe) in the bottom and whisk in the flour mixing well.

4. Cook for several minutes whisking well until it smells like popcorn and starts to turn dark blonde. Add the water and beef base. Whisk it for a minute until is thickened.

5. Add the roast, the beef base, and the carrots. Hit clear on the Instant Pot®. Place the lid on and turn the vent to pressure. Select the meat/stew switch and select high pressure. Change the time to 90 minutes.

6. Let the Instant Pot® finish it's cycle and let it bleed off naturally. Vent any remaining pressure and open the lid. Serve over potatoes or rice.

Cheesy Cauliflower

This white cheese sauce is the basis of a lot of my recipes. It is a good one to learn.

2 lbs. cauliflower, cut into bite-sized pieces

2 tsp. sea salt

½ cup water

4 Tbsp. real butter

4 Tbsp. flour

4 cups milk (whole milk is preferred)

½ pint heavy cream

½ lb. American Cheese, cut into cubes (like Velveeta or similar)

½ lb. shredded cheddar or mixed cheese like Mexican blend

Salt and pepper to taste

1. Begin by putting the cauliflower, salt, and water into the Instant Pot®. Place the lid on and set it to manual pressure high for 5 minutes. Bleed it off manually. Drain the cauliflower and set to the side.

2. Turn the Instant Pot® onto sauté. Place the butter in the bottom. Add the flour and whisk it in until the flour is well incorporated and starts to turn blonde and smell like popcorn. Pour in the milk slowly and whisk it well.

3. Place the lid on and select manual pressure low for 5 minutes. Let it bleed off naturally. Whisk it very well and slowly fold in the cream.

4. Add the cheese a little at a time and fold it in. Add the salt and pepper to taste. Fold the cauliflower into the cheese sauce and let it stand for 5 minutes before serving.

Roasted Chicken

This works best with young roasting hens. The Instant Pot® cooks them quick and has a texture similar to a rotisserie chicken.

2-4 lb. whole roasting hen, giblets removed (if any)

¼ cup olive oil

Seasoned salt to cover

Orange marmalade for glaze

2 cloves garlic, peeled and kept whole

2 fresh lemon slices

Coarse ground black pepper

1 cup chicken stock

1 Tbsp. cornstarch

4 Tbsp. real butter

1. Press sauté on the Instant Pot®, and add olive oil to the bottom of the pan. When the oil is hot, brown the chicken on all sides as best as you can.

2. Set the chicken aside on a plate, add the remaining ingredients except the marmalade and seasoned salt, to the bottom of the Instant Pot®.

3. Using a plastic or wooden scraper, scrape the bottom to deglaze the pan. Place the trivet in the Instant Pot®.

4. Using a basting brush, brush the chicken all over with the marmalade and sprinkle the seasoning salt on top until it covers it evenly, but sparsely.

5. Place the chicken, legs down, on the trivet. Close the lid, set to poultry high and set the time for 20 minutes.

6. Let the pressure bleed off naturally, remove the garlic and lemon, whisk together the sauce, carve the chicken and drizzle the sauce over the top.

Mesquite Pork Tenderloin

This is a recipe I came up with years ago for a dutch oven cooking demo. It has become one of my favorite recipes since, because of its simplicity and flavor.

1 (3-4 lb.) package pork tenderloins

1 package McCormick's Mesquite marinade mix

½ cup Worcestershire sauce

½ cup real butter

2 garlic cloves, sliced large

Olive or canola oil

1. Press sauté on the Instant Pot®, and add a little oil to the bottom of the pot. When the oil is hot, thoroughly brown the tenderloins on all sides.

2. Remove the tenderloins, and coat thoroughly with the dry mesquite seasoning.

3. Add the Worcestershire sauce, butter, and garlic to the bottom of the pot, then using a wooden or plastic scraper, scrape the bottom.

4. lace the trivet in the bottom, put the tenderloins on top, and close the lid. Set to meat, high and the time for 10 minutes.

5. Bleed the pressure off manually, remove the tenderloins and the trivet, let them relax, slice into medallions, and return to the sauce. Toss it, remove from the pot, and serve.

Maple Glazed Salmon

I really like the sweetness and flavor of real maple syrup with salmon. The Instant Pot® cooks this super fast.

Salmon cut into two 6-ounce portions, skin on

¼ cup pure maple syrup

1 tsp. black pepper

1 tsp. sea salt

½ cup water

1. Put the water in the bottom of the Instant Pot®, place the trivet inside, cover the trivet in foil, then set the two fillets on top of the foil, skin side down.

2. Brush with the maple syrup, and sprinkle the salt and pepper.

3. Place the lid on, select manual pressure high, and cook for 3 minutes. Bleed the pressure off manually, remove the fish, and enjoy.

30 min prep

about 2 hrs. total

Cola Sirloin Tips

This is a recipe I used to make a lot. It is a great-tasting, easy-to-make, hearty dish.

3 lbs. sirloin steak, cut into bite-sized cubes

1 lb. brown mushrooms, sliced

3 cloves garlic, minced

½ cup cola (not diet)

5 Tbsp. real butter

5 Tbsp. flour or cornstarch

2 cups water

1 Tbsp. beef base

Salt to taste

2 tsp. coarse ground black pepper

1. Set the Instant Pot® to sauté, and select the high option. Add a small amount of oil, brown the sirloin well, and remove from the pan.

2. Melt the butter in the bottom and whisk in the flour mixing well. Cook for several minutes whisking well until it smells like popcorn and starts to turn dark blonde.

3. Add the water, cola, and beef base. Whisk it for a minute until is thickened. Cook for several minutes.

4. Add mushrooms, beef, garlic, and pepper. Place the lid on, select manual pressure high, and set the time for 40 minutes. Let the pressure release naturally, stir well, and serve over rice or noodles.

mashed potatoes would be better

Brown Butter Vegetables

We started cooking this years ago in a dutch oven, and it has become one of my favorite ways to cook vegetables by far. The vegetables that work with it are peas, carrots, corn, and green beans, or a combination of those.

2 sticks real butter

1 (2-lb.) bag frozen vegetables
(peas, carrots, corn)

½ cup water

1. Put the butter in the Instant Pot®, turn on to sauté high, then stir the butter until it becomes brown in color and smells like popcorn.

2. Add the frozen vegetables, then the water, and fold in the butter.

3. Place the lid on, select manual high pressure, set time for five minutes. Bleed off manually and serve.

Roasted Tri-Tip

Tri-tip is one of our favorites to eat. We like it served covered in brown sauce (page 3) or in sandwiches. This is a very fast way to make tri-tip.

¼ cup canola oil

2 lbs. tri-tip roast

2 tsp. coarse ground black pepper

2 tsp. sea salt

½ cup Worcestershire sauce

4 Tbsp. real butter

¼ cup A-1 steak sauce

1. Place the canola oil in the bottom of the Instant Pot®, and select sauté high. When the oil is hot, brown the tri-tip on all sides, remove from the pan, coat with the salt and pepper evenly, and set aside.

2. Add the remaining ingredients to the Instant Pot®, and scrape the bottom with a wooden or plastic scraper.

3. Place the trivet in the bottom, set the tri-tip on the trivet, and place the lid on the Instant Pot®. Select meat, stew, and set the time for 20 minutes. Check the temperature; it should be between 125-130 degrees. If not add more time.

4. Bleed the pressure manually, remove the tri-tip, and let it stand for ten minutes. Slice thin against the grain, and drizzle with the sauce from the bottom of the pan and serve.

SOUTHERN-STYLE GREENS | PAGE 36

OLD-STYLE MACARONI AND CHEESE | PAGE 40

GUMBO | PAGE 46

CHAPTER 3:
Southern Recipes

I love Southern food. It may not be the healthiest food for you, but you can't argue with the wonderful flavors and comfort of this food. Pressure cookers have never really been explored in this realm, and it was a lot of fun for me to explore this and create new and fast ways to cook these items.

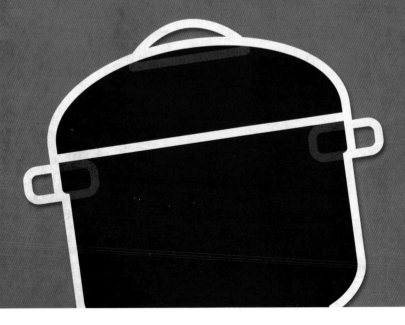

Buttermilk Fried Chicken

Colonel sanders made pressure-cooking chicken an art with his secret recipe. The advantage of pressure cooking is that you can cook the chicken all the way through without overcooking the skin and coating.

Canola oil

4 cups flour

3 tsp. salt

2 tsp. black pepper

2 tsp. smoked sweet paprika

1 tsp. onion powder

Up to 5 lbs. chicken, legs and thighs

1 quart buttermilk

1 cup panko bread crumbs

1. Fill the Instant Pot® ⅓ the way full of canola oil and select sauté and let it heat up.

2. In a bowl, mix the flour and spices together. Roll all the chicken pieces in the flour and spices and set aside on a plate.

3. Pour the buttermilk into a shallow bowl and fold the panko breadcrumbs into the remaining flour and seasoning mix.

4. Individually quickly dunk the chicken pieces into the buttermilk, let it drip a little, then roll it into the panko and flour mix and set aside.

5. Slowly lower each piece of chicken into the hot oil, making sure there is plenty of space between chicken pieces (this may take several cooking sessions). Close the lid, select manual pressure high, and set the time for twelve minutes. Bleed off the pressure manually.

6. Insert an instant read thermometer towards the bone, making sure the chicken is hotter than 165 degrees, but less than 180 (you may need to adjust your time accordingly to meet that window of temperature). Let the chicken stand on a cooling rack or paper towel for several minutes before eating.

Chicken and Dumplings

This was one recipe I wasn't quite sure how well it would work out under pressure. It turns out it works quite well. This was one of the better Chicken and Dumplings I have ever had, and it was so easy and fast to make.

5 Tbsp. real butter

5 Tbsp. flour

¾ cup onions diced small

2 cups water

2 Tbsp. chicken base

2 tsp. coarse ground black pepper

¾ cup frozen peas

¾ cup frozen carrot slices

1 rotisserie chicken cut up into bite size pieces (you can use fresh cut chicken as well, 2 cups worth)

1 can of buttermilk pop up biscuits (you can make scratch biscuits as well)

Up to 2 cups half and half, if needed for consistency

1. Press sauté on the Instant Pot® and add the butter and flour to the pan. Whisk until it is incorporated.

2. Add the onions and cook until the butter and flour is dark blonde in color and smells like popcorn. Add the water and stir well until thickened.

3. Add the remaining ingredients except the biscuits. Stir well until it is thickened and mixed thoroughly. Add half and half if needed to get the stew texture you want for the meal. Open the biscuits and layer on top until it is covered. Close the lid, hit cancel, and turn the Instant Pot® on to stew/meat. Let it finish its cycle and bleed off naturally. Serve.

Southern-Style Greens

I love greens, whether they are turnip, mustard, or collard greens. They are very good for you, providing a lot of iron, and taste amazing. The pressure cooker is the way to do it, turning a half a day chore into an hour.

3-4 lbs. of greens (can be collard, mustard, or turnip greens)

1 onion, peeled and left whole

½ cup cider vinegar

1 Tbsp. salt

1 tsp. black pepper

2 Tbsp. Louisiana-style pepper sauce

1 lb. bacon ends and pieces (or diced bacon)

3 cups water

1. Rinse the greens and roll every leaf between your palms vigorously until they turn a darker green. This will break down some of the fibers and bring out the sweetness in the greens.

2. Add all the ingredients to the Instant Pot®, close the lid, select manual pressure high and set the timer for one hour.

3. Let the greens bleed off pressure naturally and continue to cook slowly for thirty minutes. Open the lid, stir well, and serve.

Chuck Wagon-Style Beans

This is one of my most requested dishes for catering. The Instant Pot® makes quick work of this. Usually it takes all day to cook and have the flavors turn out right. With the Instant Pot®, this can be accomplished in thirty minutes.

1 lb. smoked sausage, cut into small pieces

4 (14-oz.) cans pinto beans, drained and rinsed

2 bay leaves

¼ cup honey

¼ cup barbecue sauce

2 (14-oz.) cans chicken broth

¼ cup brown sugar, packed

4 Tbsp. cider vinegar

Salt to taste

1. Add all the ingredients to the Instant Pot®, place the lid on, select beans/chili, high, and set the time for thirty minutes. Let the pressure drain off naturally and serve.

Sweet Cornbread Cakes

I love good cornbread. This is one of my favorite recipes, and one that we use in our ward cook-offs almost every year.

1½ cups yellow cornmeal

2½ cups milk

1½ cups white flour

1½ tsp. baking powder

1½ tsp. baking soda

1½ tsp. cream of tartar

2 tsp. salt

½ cup white sugar

½ cup brown sugar, packed

3 large eggs

1 stick butter, melted

1. Mix all ingredients together with a whisk, and then pour into greased ramekins or a 7-inch cake pan. Pour 1 cup water into the bottom of the Instant Pot®. Place the trivet in the bottom, set the ramekins (or cake pan) onto the trivet, put the lid on, and set the Instant Pot® to manual pressure high.

2. Cook for 15 minutes. Bleed off the pressure manually and repeat the process with any remaining batter.

Southern Creamed Corn

I never did like the canned cream corn growing up. It wasn't until I visited the south and tasted real creamed corn, that I understood what the fuss was all about.

3 Tbsp. butter

3 Tbsp. flour

1 cup milk

2 tsp. sugar

1 (16-ounce) package frozen sweet corn

1 pint heavy cream

1 tsp. salt

1. Melt the butter in the bottom of the Instant Pot®, selected to sauté. Whisk the flour in, until it is well coated with the butter. Continue stirring until the butter has a popcorn smell to it.

2. Pour in the milk and stir it in well. Add the remaining ingredients and fold in. Close the lid, select manual pressure, high, and cook for five minutes. Release the pressure manually, stir well, and serve.

Old-Style Macaroni and Cheese

This recipe is as old as America itself. It's said that Thomas Jefferson loved his "Cheesy Pasta." The Instant Pot® makes it easy.

4 Tbsp. real butter

4 Tbsp. flour

4 cups milk (whole milk is preferred)

1 lb. elbow macaroni noodles, cooked and rinsed

½ pint heavy cream

½ lb. American Cheese, cut into cubes (like Velveeta or similar)

½ lb. shredded cheddar or mixed cheese like Mexican blend

Salt and pepper to taste

1. Turn the Instant Pot® onto sauté. Place the butter in the bottom. Add the flour and whisk it in until the flour is well incorporated and starts to turn blonde and smell like popcorn.

2. Pour in the milk slowly and whisk it well. Place the lid on and select manual pressure low for 5 minutes. Let it bleed off naturally.

3. Whisk it very well and slowly fold in the cream. Add the cheese a little at a time and fold it in. Add the salt and pepper to taste. Add the cooked pasta and fold it into the cheese sauce.

Quick Brisket

Brisket is always tasty, even if this is a non-traditional way to make it. You can slice this for sandwiches or pull it and just eat it.

¼ cup canola oil

5 lbs. brisket, flat cut into large chunks

3 tsp. coarse ground black pepper

3 tsp. sea salt

½ cup barbecue sauce

4 Tbsp. real butter

¼ cup Worcestershire sauce

2 Tbsp. liquid smoke mesquite

1. Place the canola oil in the bottom of the Instant Pot®, select sauté high. When the oil is hot, brown the brisket chunks, remove from the pan, coat with the salt and pepper evenly, and set aside.

2. Add the remaining ingredients to the Instant Pot®, and scrape the bottom with a wooden or plastic scraper. Return the meat and place the lid on the Instant Pot®.

3. Select meat, stew, and set the time for 60 minutes. Bleed the pressure naturally and let it stand for 20 minutes. Slice thin against the grain, and drizzle with the sauce from the bottom or pull it and toss it in the sauce.

Roasted Pork Shoulder

I know I will get a lot of flack for this being a barbecue guy, but, in a pinch, this makes a great tender roasted pork that you can season with barbecue sauce for a sandwich or whatever you would like.

¼ cup canola oil

1 (5-lb.) boneless pork shoulder, cut into large chunks

3 tsp. coarse ground black pepper

4 tsp. sea salt

4 Tbsp. real butter

½ cup water

1. Place the canola oil in the bottom of the Instant Pot®, select sauté high. When the oil is hot, brown the pork chops, remove from the pan, coat with the salt and pepper evenly, and set aside.

2. Add the remaining ingredients to the Instant Pot®, and scrape the bottom with a wooden or plastic scraper.

3. Return the meat, and place the lid on the Instant Pot®. Select meat, stew, and set the time for 90 minutes. Bleed the pressure naturally. Remove the lid and shred the pork. Toss the shredded pork in the sauce until covered.

Southern Meatloaf

I'm not usually a fan of meatloaf, but this is one version that I enjoy.

1 onion, diced small

3 Tbsp. real butter

2 lbs. ground beef

1 lb. breakfast sausage

½ lb. ground bacon (optional)

2 cups panko bread crumbs

½ cup heavy cream

2 tsp. coarse black pepper

3 tsp. sea salt

1 Tbsp. liquid smoke

1 tsp. smoked sweet paprika

1 cup barbecue sauce

½ cup Worcestershire sauce

½ cup water

1. Begin by sautéing the onions in butter in the bottom of the Instant Pot® until they are browned. Remove from the Instant Pot®.

2. Mix the beef, sausage, bacon, onions, bread crumbs, cream, eggs, salt, pepper, liquid smoke, and paprika together in a bowl. Form into a ball or roll that will fit into the Instant Pot®.

3. Pour the barbecue sauce, Worcestershire sauce, and water into the Instant Pot®. Set the trivet inside and place a piece of foil on the trivet. Set the meat loaf down on the foil.

4. Place the lid on and set the Instant Pot® to meat/stew and the timer for 45 minutes. Let the pressure bleed off naturally and baste the meat loaf with the juices. Check the internal temperature, it should be at 155. Let it stand and relax for at least 10 minutes. Drizzle the sauce over the meatloaf once you slice it.

Rib Tips in BBQ Sauce

Rib tips are the bottom section of the spare ribs when trimmed for St. Louis ribs. The rib tips are thick and meaty with a lot of cartilage and collagen. When it is cooked right, it is absolutely delish!

¼ cup canola oil

3 lbs. rib tips, trimmed to fit in the Instant Pot®

½ cup barbecue sauce

4 Tbsp. real butter

½ cup water

3 tsp. coarse ground black pepper

4 tsp. sea salt

1. Place the canola oil in the bottom of the Instant Pot®, and select sauté high. When the oil is hot, brown the rib tips, remove from the pan, coat with the salt and pepper evenly, and set aside.

2. Add the remaining ingredients to the Instant Pot®, and scrape the bottom with a wooden or plastic scraper.

3. Return the meat, and place the lid on the Instant Pot®. Select meat, stew, and set the time for 90 minutes. Bleed the pressure naturally. Remove the lid and toss the rib tips in the sauce until covered.

Gumbo

The gumbo recipes are as diverse as the people who have perfected them. Most of the recipes have been passed down from generation to generation. There is no wrong ingredient in Gumbo. This recipe is just a base. Feel free to experiment from here. Serve with rice stirred in.

1 lb. bacon, diced

1 lb. kielbasa sausage, sliced

1 lb. chicken, beef, or peeled shrimp, cubed

1 large onion, cut into slivers

½ cup carrots, sliced

½ cup celery, sliced

½ cup okra, sliced

2 sticks real butter

1 cup flour

6 cups beef stock

3 tsp. coarse black pepper

2 tsp. sea salt

4 bay leaves

(optional) 3 Tbsp. hot sauce

1. Begin by selecting sauté on the Instant Pot®. Brown the bacon and remove. Brown the kielbasa and your choice of meat and remove.

2. Add the onions, carrots, and celery, cook until brown. Add the okra and cook for 2 minutes. Set the veggies aside with the meat.

3. Stir in the butter and the flour and stir constantly until it is a rich reddish-brown color and smells very nutty. Stir in the beef base immediately and stir until thickened. Add the remaining ingredients and return the meat and veggies.

4. Place the lid on and set the pot to soup and the time for 30 minutes. Let the pressure release naturally. Serve with cooked rice stirred in. You can garnish with powdered filet or sassafras leaf (found in the spice aisle of some stores) for an authentic taste.

Glazed Pork Belly

Most people are familiar with pork belly as bacon. Uncured fresh pork belly is a very tasty treat. It is rich, tender, and juicy meat. It usually takes hours and hours to cook right. The Instant Pot® makes this treat much quicker.

3-4 lbs. fresh pork belly, cut to fit into the pot

¼ cup canola oil

1 small jar orange marmalade

1 cup apple juice

1 tsp. liquid smoke hickory flavor

3 tsp. black pepper

2 tsp. sea salt

2 tsp. smoked sweet paprika

1. Begin by selecting sauté high on the Instant Pot®. Pour the oil in and wait until it is hot. Brown the belly pieces very well on all sides.

2. Remove from the pot and completely coat with the marmalade. Pour the apple juice and liquid smoke in the Instant Pot®. Scrape the bottom with a wooden or plastic scraper. Sprinkle the pepper, salt, and paprika on the bellies.

3. Place the trivet in the bottom of the pot and set the bellies on top. Put the lid and seat to meat/stew and set the time for 90 minutes. Let the pressure bleed off manually and sit for 20 minutes. Open the lid and remove the bellies. Slice the bellies against the grain and drizzle with the sauce to serve.

CHEDDAR BROCCOLI SOUP | PAGE 50

CHICKEN AND WILD RICE SOUP | PAGE 55

BEST DARN CHILI | PAGE 53

CHAPTER 4:
Soups, Stews, and Chilis

Everywhere I worked as a chef, I became famous for making my soups and stews. I never thought there was anything special about what I did. There is some magic that can happen though when following a process and making a good soup. The Instant Pot® lends itself well to soups and stews. The pressure cooking gives it a "next day" flavor.

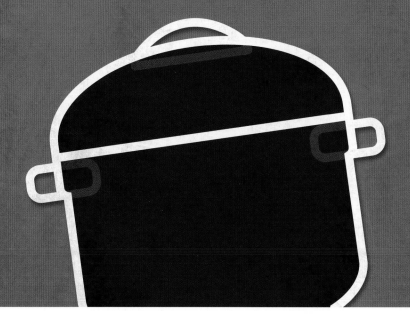

Cheddar Broccoli Soup

This is an amazingly good version of this soup. It goes great with fresh-made rolls or breadsticks.

3 cups water

1 Tbsp. salt

1 lb. broccoli florets

4 Tbsp. real butter

4 Tbsp. flour

2 cups milk

1 cup half and half

1 tsp. black pepper

2 tsp. sea salt

1 lb. shredded cheddar cheese

½ pint heavy cream

1. Add three cups water and one Tbsp. full of salt to the Instant Pot®. Select sauté high and wait for it to boil. Drop the broccoli florets and stir in the boiling water for two minutes. Remove and rinse in cold water or ice bath to stop cooking. Set it aside.

2. Drain the water from the Instant Pot® and dry out. Add the butter and flour to the Instant Pot®, select sauté and whisk the butter and flour until incorporated. Stir as it cooks until it becomes blonde in color and smells of buttered popcorn.

3. Add the milk, half and half, and salt and pepper. Stir until it is thickened. Hit the clear button on the Instant Pot®, select the slow cooker mode, and let the soup cook for 20–30 minutes. Slowly stir in the cheese a little at a time until incorporated. Stir in the cream and slowly fold the broccoli in and serve.

Tomato Basil Soup

This is my favorite soup to dip a grilled cheese sandwich in. It's made from fresh tomatoes and normally takes quite a while to make. The Instant Pot® makes it so much easier to make.

6 Tbsp. real butter

½ cup onions diced small

4 Tbsp. flour or cornstarch

2 (28-oz.) cans of crushed tomatoes

2 Tbsp. chicken base

3 bay leaves

4 cups diced fresh tomatoes

3 cups heavy cream

1 cup grated Romano cheese

6-8 leaves fresh basil torn by hand

Salt and pepper to taste

1. Place the Butter in the Instant Pot® and turn the pot on to sauté. Add the onions and stir in the butter until the onions are clear. Stir in the flour and cook it stirring frequently until the flour is starting to turn blonde and smells like popcorn.

2. Add the crushed and fresh tomatoes. Stir in well and add the chicken base and bay leaves. Put the lid on, hit cancel, and turn it on to stew/meat. Let the soup finish the cycle. Bleed it off quickly, stir the soup taking care to scrape the bottom with a wooden utensil.

3. Add the cream slowly and stirring frequently. Remove the bay leaves and slowly stir in the basil and the Romano cheese. Blend the soup up with an immersion blender and serve.

Ham and White Bean Soup

This is my favorite cold weather meal. Traditionally this takes hours to make properly. With the Instant Pot®, I can make this in 30 minutes.

1 lb. diced ham cubes

1 small onion, kept whole and peeled

4 cups water

3 (14-oz.) cans of great northern beans, drained and rinsed

3 bay leaves

2 Tbsp. chicken base

Salt and pepper to taste

1. Add all the ingredients to Instant Pot®, close the lid, select meat/stew. Let it cook the full cycle for 30 minutes. Let it bleed off naturally. Remove the bay leaves and onion, and add salt and pepper to taste.

Best Darn Chili

This is one of my favorite chili recipes and my go to anytime we want chili as a family. The Instant Pot® makes quick work of this recipe and gives you that "next day" flavor deep into the beans.

1 lb. beef or pork, cut into small bite size chunks

1 lb. smoked sausage or kielbasa, sliced into bite size pieces

2 (14-oz.) cans of pinto beans, rinsed and drained

1 (14-oz.) can of black beans, rinsed and drained

1 (28-oz.) can crushed tomatoes

1 Tbsp. beef base

¼ cup cider vinegar

½ cup brown sugar, packed

1 (2-oz.) can mild diced green chiles

2 poblano peppers, seeded and rinsed, diced fine

1 large onion, kept whole with paper removed

3 cloves garlic, peeled and crushed

¼ cup barbecue sauce

2 tsp. chili powder

Salt and pepper to taste

(optional) 1 cup crushed tortilla chips to thicken

1. Add all of the ingredients to the Instant Pot®. Place the lid on and seal it. Turn the Pot on to the Beans/Chili cycle. Let it finish the cycle and bleed off naturally.

2. Remove the onion, and stir it well. Thicken with corn tortilla chips if you want it thickened. Garnish with cheese and green onions and serve.

Award-Winning Chili

This is my winningest chili recipe. I cook this all the time for chili contests and it almost always wins. This year I cooked it in the Instant Pot® just to see how it would do. It won first place and it only took an hour and a half in total. Enjoy!

3 lbs. beef chuck roast, cut into bite-sized cubes

1 lb. polish sausage, cut up into slices

1 large yellow sweet onion, diced

6 cloves garlic, peeled and left whole

3 Chili Guanjillos, seeds removed and rinsed (this is a dried chile available in Latin markets)

3 New Mexico chiles, seeds removed and rinsed

1 cup Tampico citrus juice or Sunny D

3 Tbsp. Beef Base

2 bay leaves

2 limes, juiced and zested

¼ cup cider vinegar

Salt to taste

2 tsp. of cumin

2 (14-oz.) cans pinto beans, drained and rinsed

1 (14-oz.) can black beans, drained and rinsed

1. Add a little oil in the bottom of the Instant Pot® and turn it to sauté high. Brown the meat a little at a time and set aside on a plate.

2. Add the onions, cook until clear. Add the remaining ingredients except the beef, sausage, and beans. Place the lid on, set the Instant Pot® to manual high, and set the time for 15 minutes. Release the pressure manually and open the lid. Drain any juice from resting the meat into the pot.

3. With an immersion blender, blend the contents of the pot until it is smooth in consistency. Add the salt to taste. Add the beef, sausage, and beans, and stir it in so that it is covered with the sauce. Replace the lid and turn the Instant Pot® on beans/chili for 45 minutes. Release the pressure manually and serve. Garnish with corn tortillas and fresh cilantro.

Chicken and Wild Rice Soup

This recipe is one of my favorites. You can use leftover turkey instead of chicken for the protein, and if you prefer you can use white rice instead of wild rice.

1 cup wild rice medley

1 cup water

1 tsp. sea salt

½ cup real butter

1 medium onion, ¼-inch diced

2 cups carrots, sliced

2 cups celery, sliced

3 cloves garlic, minced

6 Tbsp. flour

6 cups chicken stock

3 lbs. rotisserie chicken or leftover turkey, pulled and chopped

3 bay leaves

1 tsp. white pepper

2 tsp. black pepper

1 tsp. paprika

2 Tbsp. chicken base

1 cup heavy cream (optional)

1. Begin by putting the wild rice, water, and salt in the Instant Pot®. Close the lid and select the rice function. Let the pot bleed off naturally. Remove the rice from the pot and set to the side.

2. Select sauté on the Instant Pot® and put the butter in the bottom and melt it. Add the onions, carrots, and celery, and cook until the onions are clear. Add the minced garlic and stir in the flour. Stir it in well until the flour is well coated and saturated.

3. Pour the chicken stock in and stir it well. Add the chicken, bay leaves, pepper, paprika, rice, and chicken base. Close the lid and select the soup function and set the time for 15 minutes. Let the pressure bleed off naturally.

4. Open the Instant Pot® and stir well taking special care to stir the bottom. Add the cream and slowly fold in before serving.

Mulligatawny

This recipe is my favorite soup bar none. It originated in India with the English that lived there combining their two cultures for a creamy rice and curry soup.

2 cups white rice

2 cups water

1 tsp. sea salt

½ cup real butter

1 medium onion, ¼-inch diced

2 cups carrots, sliced

2 cups celery, sliced

3 cloves garlic, minced

6 Tbsp. flour

4 cups chicken stock

3 lbs. rotisserie chicken or leftover turkey, pulled and chopped

3 bay leaves

1 tsp. white pepper

2 tsp. black pepper

1 tsp. thyme

1 cup masala curry simmer sauce

2 Tbsp. chicken base

2 cups heavy cream

2 cups granny smith apples cored and cut into small chucks

Sea salt to taste

1. Begin by putting the rice, water, and salt in the Instant Pot®. Close the lid and select the rice function. Let the pot bleed off naturally. Remove the rice from the pot and set to the side.

2. Select sauté on the Instant Pot® and put the butter in the bottom and melt it. Add the onions, carrots, and celery, and cook until the onions are clear. Add the minced garlic and stir in the flour. Stir it in well until the flour is well coated and saturated.

3. Pour the chicken stock in and stir it well. Add the chicken, bay leaves, pepper, thyme, curry simmer sauce, and chicken base. Close the lid and select the soup function and set the time for 15 minutes. Let the pressure bleed off naturally.

4. Open the Instant Pot® and stir well taking special care to stir the bottom. Add the cream. Apples, and rice. Slowly fold it all together and let it relax for 10 minutes before serving.

Roasted Red Pepper Soup

This is a creamy base soup with a very pleasant flavor. You can add meat to it if you want to but it's not necessary. I like to serve it with a grilled cheese sandwich.

5 red bell peppers, seeds removed and rinsed

¼ cup canola oil

1 cup sweet onions, diced small

½ cup carrots, diced

½ cup celery, diced

½ cup real butter

6 Tbsp. flour

4 cups vegetable or chicken stock

½ cup brown mushrooms, cut small

½ cup roma tomatoes, diced

3 bay leaves

2 tsp. black pepper

1 pint heavy cream

½ cup parmesan cheese, shredded

Sea salt to taste

1. Begin by placing the red bell peppers and oil in the Instant Pot® and turn it on to sauté high. Cook until the peppers are starting to bubble and turn brown on the skin. Remove from the pot and set aside.

2. Add the onions, carrots, and celery. Cook until they onions are clear. Add the butter and stir until melted. Add the flour and stir it in until it is well incorporated and coated completely. Add the stock, mushrooms, tomatoes, and bay leaves.

3. Peel the bell peppers as well as you can and add them with the black pepper. Place the lid on the Instant Pot®, select soup, and set the time for 20 minutes. Let the pressure bleed off naturally.

4. Open the lid and stir everything well. Slowly add the cream and parmesan a little at a time. Remove the bay leaves. With an immersion blender, blend the soup very well until smooth and creamy. Add the salt to taste. Garnish with chicken and cheese if desired.

MOLE | PAGE 67

REFRIED BEANS FROM SCRATCH | PAGE 66

POZOLE | PAGE 69

CHAPTER 5:
Mexican Recipes

I've been asked often, if I could only choose one type of cuisine for the rest of my life, what would it be? Though I could never imagine such a scenario, I would have to say Mexican food may be it. I love the rich complexities of flavors and basic food items. These recipes have all turned out really good cooked under pressure. They have been definite crowd pleasers.

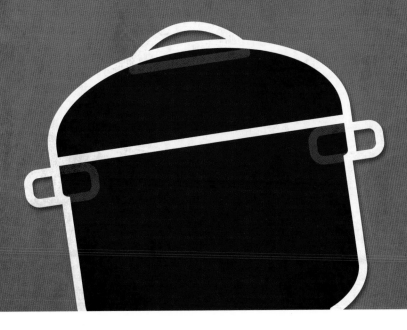

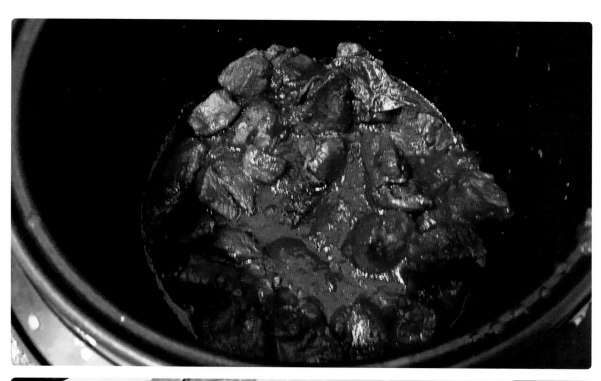

Birria (Barbacoa)

This traditional Mexican braised meat dish is extremely popular at weddings, funerals, and parties. It is mislabeled as barbacoa here in the US but it is properly known as Birria in Mexico, Barbacoa being something completely different. It can be served in bowls or on a plate as a thick stew or in tortillas as tacos, etc. This is one of my most often requested recipe when I cook it for a group. This recipe calls for beef, but it can be made with lamb, goat, or venison as well.

5 lbs. of beef chuck roast, cut into large cubes

1 large yellow sweet onion, diced

6 cloves of garlic, peeled and left whole

3 Chili Guanjillos, seeds removed and rinsed (this is a dried chile available in latin markets)

3 New Mexico chiles, seeds removed and rinsed

1 cup Tampico citrus juice or Sunny D

3 Tbsp. beef base

2 bay leaves

2 limes, juiced and zested

¼ cup cider vinegar

Salt to taste

1. Add a little oil in the bottom of the Instant Pot® and turn it to sauté high. Brown the meat a little at a time and set aside on a plate.

2. Add the onions, cook until clear. Add the remaining ingredients except the beef. Place the lid on and set the Instant Pot® to manual high and set the time for 15 minutes. Release the pressure manually and open the lid. Drain any juice from resting the meat into the pot.

3. With an immersion blender, blend the contents of the pot until it is smooth in consistency. Add the salt to taste. Add the beef and stir it in so that it is covered with the sauce. Replace the lid and turn the Instant Pot® on manual high for 45 minutes. Release the pressure manually and serve. Garnish with corn tortillas and fresh cilantro.

Carnitas

This traditional Mexican meat is a favorite for street tacos, enchiladas, and burritos. Very simple to make and very tasty.

5 lbs. boneless pork shoulder, cut into large cubes (do not trim fat)

1 can sweetened condensed milk

½ cup canola oil

3 tsp. salt

2 tsp. black pepper

1 cup water

1. Set the Instant Pot® to sauté and high, add the oil, and wait a few minutes until it's hot. Add the pork a few chunks at a time and brown very thoroughly. Remove and set to the side.

2. Pour in the water and using a wooden or plastic spatula, scrape the bits off the bottom of the pan and deglaze it. Add the sweetened condensed milk, and add the pork, making sure to include any drippings that stayed on the plate. Close the lid, set it on manual high for two hours.

3. Let it finish off its cycle and bleed off naturally. Stir well into the juices. Use in tacos, enchiladas, burritos, etc.

Spanish Rice

I made this recipe for the first time at a pioneer trek recreation where I was assigned to cook. It was cooked with the dutch oven with ingredients I had on hand. The recipe turned out to be a hit and everyone really liked it. I have adapted it for the Instant Pot®, which is great because of how fast it cooks.

4 cups rice

4 cups water

1 (14-oz.) can of El Pato brand green enchilada sauce

2 Tbsp. chicken base

1 tsp. onion powder

1 tsp. garlic powder

¼ cup diced carrots

¼ cup frozen peas

¼ cup frozen corn

1. Add all the ingredients to the Instant Pot® and stir it well. Set the Instant Pot® to rice and let it finish the cycle and bleed the pressure off naturally. Let it relax for 15 minutes before opening the lid. Stir it well and serve.

Chile Verde

This dish is a staple of New Mexico. Every year in late summer when the chiles are harvested, roadside vendors will roast fresh picked green chiles. You buy a bag and then the work begins of peeling and seeding the chiles so you can freeze them and have chile verde for the rest of the year. My favorite way to eat them is in enchiladas. You can use the chile verde sauce for everything as a topper, even your breakfast eggs and hash browns. The Instant Pot® makes quick work of this dish and the results are amazing.

2 lbs. pork country style ribs, cut into large bite-size chunks (you can also use boneless chicken thighs)

1 cup roasted, peeled, and diced Hatch green chiles (Anaheim or Poblano will work)

2 Tbsp. chicken base

4 Tbsp. real butter

4 Tbsp. flour or cornstarch

2 cups water

1. Set the Instant Pot® to sauté, select the high option. Melt the butter in the bottom and whisk in the flour mixing well. Cook for several minutes, whisking well until it smells like popcorn and starts to turn dark blonde.

2. Add the water, green chiles, and chicken base. Whisk it for a minute until it thickens. Add the pork.

3. Hit clear on the Instant Pot®. Place the lid on and turn the vent to pressure. Select the meat/stew switch and select high pressure. Let the Instant Pot® finish its cycle and let it bleed off naturally.

4. Vent any remaining pressure and open the lid.

5. *For Enchiladas* Wrap in tortillas with cheese and chunks of the meat, drizzle chile verde sauce over the top of individual servings, sprinkle with cheese, and place in the oven on high broil for 2-3 minutes until the cheese is bubbly.

Refried Beans from Scratch

I'm not a fan of regular canned refried beans, but I love the homemade version. These are very simple to make.

4 cans pinto beans, rinsed and drained

2 cups chicken stock

1 (2-oz.) can of medium diced green chiles

1 small onion, diced fine

½ stick real butter (4 Tbsp.)

2 tsp. sea salt

2 tsp. black pepper

1 Tbsp. honey

1 cup shredded Mexican blend cheese (optional)

1. Place all the ingredients except the cheese into the Instant Pot®. Place the lid on and set to beans/chili and set the time for 20 minutes. Let it bleed off naturally and remove the lid. Drain the liquid off the beans and set to the side.

2. Using a blender, mix the beans up adding the liquid back in until you have the desired consistency. Fold in the cheese a little at a time until you have your desired amount.

3. If you want to do this from dried beans, follow the recipe the same other than you want to soak the beans ahead of time and pull out any messed up beans. Cook for 60 minutes instead of 20 minutes.

Mole

This mole recipe is for the mole itself. Mole is a chile and chocolate sauce famous in southern Mexico. It is absolutely delicious with pork or chicken served with beans and tortillas.

1 onion, diced small

¼ cup canola oil

3 dried guanjillo chiles, seeds removed

2 dried ancho chiles, seeds removed

2 dried chipotle chiles, seeds removed

3 cloves garlic, chopped

½ cup raisins

4 oz. dark chocolate, chopped (70% or purer)

1 cup chicken stock

2 bay leaves

3 roma tomatoes, diced

½ cup tomatillos, diced

1 tsp. cinnamon

½ tsp. allspice

½ tsp. cloves

6 corn tortillas, cut into strips

Salt to taste

1. Add the canola oil and the onions to the Instant Pot®. Select sauté and cook until they are browned. Add the remaining ingredients except the tortillas.

2. Place the lid on and set the pot to manual pressure high and cook for 40 minutes. Let the pressure bleed off naturally.

3. Open the lid and stir in the tortillas, and let it sit for 10 minutes. Use an immersion blender and blend it until it is smooth. You can now cook chicken or pork in this or just set it to the side and use it to cover any protein for an authentic Mexican flavor.

Chicken Tortilla Soup

This recipe is just easy and fun. Serve over corn tortilla chips with any combination of meat, sour cream, guacamole, etc. The Instant Pot® makes it easy.

4 Tbsp. real butter

4 Tbsp. flour

6 cups milk (whole milk is preferred)

½ pint heavy cream

½ lb. American cheese, cut into cubes (like Velveeta or similar)

Salt and pepper to taste

1 cup medium spicy salsa

½ lb. shredded cheddar or mixed cheese like Mexican blend

1 tsp. cumin

½ lb. cooked chicken (pulled rotisserie works well)

6-8 corn tortillas cut into strips

tomatoes, for garnish

1. Turn the Instant Pot® onto sauté. Place the butter in the bottom. Add the flour and whisk it in until the flour is well incorporated and starts to turn blonde and smell like popcorn. Pour in the milk slowly and whisk it well.

2. Place the lid on and select soup for 10 minutes. Let it bleed off naturally. Whisk it very well and slowly fold in the cream. Add the cheese a little at a time and fold it in. Add the salt and pepper to taste.

3. Add the salsa and fold it into the cheese sauce. Fold in the cumin, chicken, and tortillas. Garnish with fresh cut tomatoes.

Pozole

This is my all-time favorite Mexican soup. I used to make it a lot, but with a busy lifestyle and little time, I have slacked off. I am pleased with the Instant Pot® because I can make it so much quicker now.

1 large sweet onion, sliced large

3 lbs. boneless pork country style ribs or pork shoulder cut into bite-sized chunks

2 (28-oz.) cans white hominy, rinsed and drained

1 (28-oz.) can crushed tomatoes

4 cups chicken stock

4 cloves garlic, sliced

3 bay leaves

1 (4-oz.) can medium diced green chiles

3 tsp. ground New Mexico chile powder

2 tsp. smoked sweet paprika

2 tsp. black pepper

¼ cup cider vinegar

1 lime squeezed

2 Tbsp. chicken base

1. Add all the ingredients to the Instant Pot®. Place the lid on, select the soup function, and set the time for 45 minutes. Let the pressure bleed off naturally.

2. Serve and garnish with Mexican table cream, Tostadas, limes, and shredded cabbage.

Tamales

Tamales are one of those dishes that when you make them, you make enough so you can freeze them and have them for later. In this recipe, I'm not specifying a protein but rather the tamale masa and the process of how to make them. You can use any of the Mexican meat dishes to place inside the tamales or you can fill them with raisins, sugar, and cinnamon for dessert tamales. One of my favorite is to fill them with fresh sweet corn and mozzarella cheese for a different spin on the traditional tamales. The Instant Pot® is perfect for cooking them fully.

2½ cups masa harina

1 tsp. salt

1½ tsp. baking powder

¾ cup lard or butter-flavored Crisco shortening

2 cups chicken broth (or warm water if you are making dessert tamales)

1 cup water

1 package dried corn husks

1. Mix the masa, salt, and baking powder together in a bowl. Whip the lard and add a little of the broth at a time until the lard is fluffy. Fold into the masa mixture and add the broth a little at a time until it is very spongy.

2. Soak the corn husks in water. Spread the masa onto the corn husks. Add the meat or filling on top of the masa, fold the corn husk, and tuck the bottom.

3. Pour the water into the Instant Pot® and place the trivet in the bottom. Place some foil on top of the trivet, lay the tamales on the trivet either vertical with the tucked end down (preferred) or stack them alternating layers.

4. Close the lid and set the Instant Pot® to manual pressure high and set the time for 20 minutes. Bleed off the pressure manually, open the lid, and let it stand for 10 minutes before removing from the pot.

CHICKEN TERIYAKI | PAGE 80

CASHEW CHICKEN | PAGE 75

PHO | PAGE 79

CHAPTER 6:
Asian
Recipes

My training as a chef began in Asian fusion cuisine. This is a genre of food I truly love. This chapter has some of my favorite recipes that adapted well to be cooked under pressure.

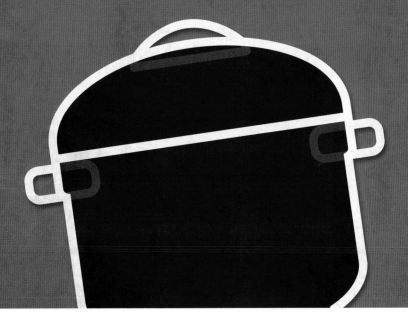

Ginger Beef and Snow Peas

This Asian-inspired dish was one of my favorites growing up. My family would cook it often and serve it over rice with chow mein noodles and egg rolls. It is extremely simple to make.

1 cup teriyaki sauce

2 tsp. fresh grated ginger

2 cloves garlic, minced

2 lbs. beef flank or skirt steak, cut into strips

2 lbs. snow peas

3 Tbsp. sesame oil

1 tsp. black pepper

1. Three hours ahead of time, mix the teriyaki sauce, ginger, black pepper, and garlic together. Add the beef and stir it well. Let it sit in the fridge until ready to cook.

2. Remove the strings from the snow peas and set aside.

3. Pour the sesame oil in the Instant Pot® and turn it onto sauté high. Using tongs, set the meat from the bowl into the pot. Stir it well until lightly browned. Add the snow peas and the remaining liquid from the meat. Close the lid and set the Instant Pot® to manual high and set the time for 10 minutes. Bleed off the pressure manually and serve over rice.

30 min · prep
30 min cook

Cashew Chicken

Over the years this has been one of my family's favorite dishes and one that was asked for a number of birthday dinners. It is relatively simple to make. You can feel free to substitute whatever vegetables you want because it really doesn't matter.

4 Tbsp. real butter

1 Tbsp. sesame oil

8 oz. salted cashew pieces

1 medium sweet onion, cut into slivers

2 lbs. chicken breasts, cut into thin strips

1 head broccoli, cut into florets
cauliflower
carrots

X 4 celery stalks, cut into slices

1 cup water

½ cup soy sauce

2 tsp. black pepper

3 Tbsp. cornstarch

(optional) bamboo shoots, water chestnuts, red bell peppers, etc.

1. Put the butter and sesame oil into the Instant Pot®. Select sauté high. Add the cashews, and stir until they are starting to brown a little. Remove the cashews from the pan and set aside.

2. Add the onions and the chicken, and stir them in until the chicken is turning white and the onions are beginning to become clear.

3. Add the remaining ingredients except the cornstarch. *not cashew mix!* Place the lid on the Instant Pot® and select meat/stew high and set the time for 5 minutes. Release the pressure manually and remove the lid.

4. Stir the cornstarch with a small amount of cold water to make a slurry. Pour the slurry into the pot until it thickens. Repeat if necessary until the desired thickness is achieved. Return the cashews to the mix and fold in. Serve over Jasmine rice.

Hawaiian Kalbi Short Ribs

These are very similar to the Korean short ribs, with the exception being pineapple. Served with rice and pasta salad traditionally.

4–5 lbs. beef short ribs

1 cup brown sugar, packed

1 cup soy sauce

¼ cup mirin sauce

1 onion, diced

6 cloves garlic, minced

3 Tbsp. dark sesame oil

1 tsp. black pepper

½ cup crushed pineapple

1 cup water

1. The night before, or at least three hours before, mix all the ingredients except for the short ribs and water, in a bowl. Whisk until the sugar is dissolved. Add the short ribs, making sure they are thoroughly covered, and place in the fridge to marinate.

2. When ready to prepare, hit sauté on the Instant Pot® and add some canola oil on the bottom. Let it get up to temperature, then brown the short ribs, one or two at a time and set aside on the plate.

3. When all are browned, place the trivet in the bottom and set the short ribs on top of the trivet.

4. Add the water to the bottom, close the lid, set the Instant Pot® to manual high pressure, and set the time for 45 minutes. Let it bleed off naturally, open the lid, remove the trivet, and cook on sauté, stirring the short ribs until the liquid level goes down and becomes sticky on the ribs. Serve and enjoy.

Thai Golden Curry

I love Thai food! Golden Curry is one of my favorites. You can use any protein you like—chicken, pork, beef, or shrimp. This recipe will call for chicken as it is the least expensive and easiest to come by. Feel free to substitute for any one though.

3 Tbsp. canola oil

2-3 lbs. chicken breasts, cut into small chunks

4 Tbsp. real butter

4 Tbsp. flour or cornstarch

¼ cup flour (set aside)

2 cups water

3 Tbsp. chicken base

2 Tbsp. or cubes of Thai Golden Curry paste

2 (14-oz.) cans of Thai coconut milk, shaken well

1 large sweet onion

2 cups carrot slices

1 (14-oz.) can of new potatoes sliced

1 (4-oz.) can of bamboo shoots

3 Tbsp. creamy peanut butter

Salt and pepper to taste

(optional) ¼ cup of golden fish sauce

1. Place the oil in the bottom of the Instant Pot®. Turn it on to sauté and high and let it heat up for a few minutes. Brown the chicken pieces lightly and remove.

2. Dust the chicken with the flour or cornstarch. Add the butter and the flour to the pan and stir well, making sure to whick the bits from the bottom of the pan. Cook until the flour turns golden blonde and smells like cooked popcorn.

3. Add the water and chicken base. Stir until the mixture is thickened. Add the curry paste and the coconut milk. Stir in until the curry is dissolved.

4. Add the remaining ingredients with the chicken on the bottom. Place the lid on the Instant Pot® and set it to the stew/meat function for 30 minutes. Let the pot finish its cycle and bleed off naturally. Serve over jasmine rice.

Pho

Of all the foods in this world, I think that pho is probably my go-to comfort food. The base is where it's at. If you have a good base the rest will be great. You can make pho out of any major protein. I am using beef in this recipe because it is the traditional. The Instant Pot® is great for making quick work of the base.

FOR THE BASE

1 large sweet onion, cut in half and peel removed

2 cups carrots, sliced

2 cups celery, sliced

4 cloves garlic, peeled and kept whole

2 cloves shallots, sliced

2 lbs. beef bones such as oxtails

4 pods star anise

2 quarts beef stock or 6 (14 oz.) cans

4 tsp. beef base

2 limes, squeezed

1 sprig Thai basil, kept whole

FOR FINISHING

2 lbs. beef round, sliced very thin

1 lb. dried rice vermicelli noodles (par boil for 2 minutes, rinse, and chill)

Green onion, cilantro, bean sprouts, jalapenos, Thai basil to garnish

1. Add all the ingredients for the base to the Instant Pot®. Place the lid on and set the pot to manual pressure high and set the time for 60 minutes. Drain the pot through a sieve and remove the solids.

2. Return the liquid to the pot and select sauté high. When the mixture is boiling, turn off the power. Ladle into serving bowls filled with chilled noodles and raw thin slices of beef. Let it relax for 5 minutes before eating. Garnish with fresh herbs and veggies.

Teriyaki Chicken

This version is the island version of Teriyaki. It is great served over rice and with a pasta salad or great served in a roll as a sandwich.

¼ cup canola oil

2-3 lbs. boneless skinless chicken thighs, with fat trimmed

1 cup teriyaki sauce (I prefer Mr. Yoshidas)

½ cup barbecue sauce (I used Sweet Baby Ray's Original)

2 tsp. liquid smoke mesquite

½ cup crushed pineapple

¼ cup water

1. Begin by adding the oil to the Instant Pot® and setting it to sauté high. When the oil is hot, brown the chicken thighs well on both sides and set them to the side.

2. Add the remaining ingredients to the pot and whisk together making sure to scrape the bottom well.

3. Return the chicken to the pot, close the lid, and select meat/stew high and set the time for 25 minutes. Bleed off the pressure manually. Serve either pulled or sliced with the sauce drizzled over the top.

Kalua Pork

This is the easiest recipe to cook. It is a very tasty way to eat pork. Whether you eat it over rice or with pasta salad or in a roll.

¼ cup canola oil

5-6 lbs. boneless pork shoulder or country style spare ribs, cut into large chunks

2 Tbsp. Hawaiian sea salt

1 Tbsp. liquid smoke mesquite

1 cup chicken stock

1. Pour the oil into the bottom of the Instant Pot®, and select sauté high. When the oil is hot, brown the pork a couple of pieces at a time. Remove the pork and set aside.

2. Add the remaining ingredients and scrape the bottom using a plastic or wooden scraper. Return the pork to the Instant Pot®, close the lid, and select meat/stew, and set the time for 60 minutes. Let the pressure bleed off naturally. Pull the pork and toss it through the sauce before serving,

Vindaloo Chicken

I am a huge fan of Indian food. This region of the world is the origin of so many spices. The sauces are complex and balanced. It's so easy nowadays to just buy Indian simmer sauces but you can't beat a from-scratch recipe. You can substitute the chicken for fish or shrimp just as easy. Just make sure to cut down the second cooking time if you do that. Serve over basmati rice for authentic cuisine or over any rice.

¼ cup canola oil

3 lbs. chicken (boneless skinless thighs or breasts), cut into chunks

2 cups chicken stock

1 stick real butter

1 large sweet onion, ¼-inch diced

4 cloves garlic, peeled and kept whole

3 tsp. powdered ginger

2 tsp. cumin

2 tsp. ground mustard seed

1 tsp. cinnamon

½ tsp. cloves

1 Tbsp. Tumeric

1 tsp. cayenne pepper (add more if spiciness is desired)

1 Tbsp. smoked sweet paprika

1 lemon squeezed

2 Tbsp. white vinegar

1 Tbsp. packed brown sugar

2 tsp. sea salt

1. Begin by pouring the canola oil in the bottom of the Instant Pot® and setting it to sauté high. When the oil is hot, cook the chicken until it is turning white. Remove from the pan and set to the side.

2. Add all the remaining ingredients, starting with the chicken stock making sure to scrape the bottom with a wooden or plastic scraper. Close the lid and set the pot to manual pressure high and set the time for 10 minutes. Manually release the pressure and open the lid.

3. Using an immersion blender, mix up the contents until smooth. Add the chicken back in, close the lid, and set the pot to meat/stew and set the time for 20 minutes. Let the pressure bleed off naturally. Stir the vindaloo well and serve over rice.

LASAGNA | PAGE 91

BEEF BOURGUIGNON | PAGE 92

CHICKEN GNOCCHI SOUP | PAGE 95

CHAPTER 7:
French, Italian, and German Recipes

I struggled with what to call this section, even contemplating calling it European recipes. These are some of my favorite dishes from that side of the world. A lot of the basics that I cook come from these regions.

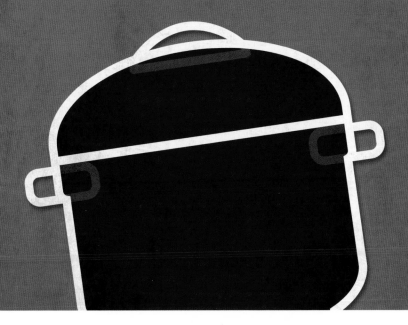

Italian Meatballs

Use this recipes with the fresh marinara sauce for spaghetti with meatballs or meatball subs. These are so simple to make and the Instant Pot® is the perfect tool to make them quickly.

2 lbs. ground sweet Italian sausage

4 eggs, beaten

2 cups panko bread crumbs

¼ cup olive oil

4 cups fresh marinara sauce

1. Mix the sausage, eggs, and bread crumbs together in a bowl. Roll into even (about 4 oz. or a small ice cream scoop) balls and set aside.

2. Place the olive oil in the bottom of the Instant Pot®. Push the sauté high button on the Instant Pot®. When the oil starts to shimmer, place the meatballs in the bottom. Brown them on all sides.

3. Add the marinara sauce. Place the lid on the Instant Pot® and turn the Instant Pot® on meat/stew and set the time for 20 minutes. Let it finish its cycle and bleed it off.

4. Serve with fresh sliced mozzarella on a hard roll for a meatball sandwich or serve over noodles with fresh grated cheese for spaghetti and meatballs.

From Scratch Marinara Sauce

Nothing beats a fresh-made marinara sauce from garden fresh ingredients. You can make large amounts ahead of time and bottle them or freeze them for later use. You can also use it for pizza, spaghetti, and meatballs, or a meatball sub sandwich.

¼ cup olive oil

1 lb. pancetta or bacon, diced

1 large sweet onion, ¼-inch diced (about 1½ cups)

1 cup celery, ¼-inch diced

1 cup carrots, sliced small

1 (28-oz.) can stewed tomatoes

4 cups fresh tomatoes, diced

6 cloves garlic, peeled and crushed

3 bay leaves, crushed

1 cup white grape juice

2 Tbsp. fresh oregano

2 tsp. baking soda

Salt and pepper to taste

1. Pour the olive oil into the bottom of the Instant Pot® and let it coat the bottom. Select sauté, add the bacon, and brown the bacon well. Add the onions and stir in until they are fully coated with oil. Cook until the onions are clear.

2. Add the carrots and celery, and cook until the carrots start to sweat. Add the tomatoes, garlic, bay leaves, and white grape juice. Press cancel, put on the lid, and hit the soup function on the Instant Pot®. When the pot finishes the cycle, crack the valve and bleed the pressure.

3. Open the lid and add the oregano and baking soda. Using an immersion blender, blend thoroughly until smooth. Add the salt and pepper to taste. If desired, you can add grated Parmesan or Romano cheese to the sauce once the sauce has cooled down.

Lasagna

I was skeptical at first. I've always made a lot of lasagnas in the oven or the dutch oven but the thought of doing it in a pressure cooker seemed like a challenge to me. It posed a challenge, but a successful one. Even though you don't get the crispiness of an oven-baked lasagna or the bubbly cheese, you get a nice lasagna fast with the same "next day" flavor, you would get on a traditional lasagna dish.

1 package oven ready lasagna noodles

2 lbs. cut meatballs (recipe page 105) or sweet Italian sausage browned

2 lbs. shredded mozzarella cheese

32 oz. part skim ricotta cheese

2 cups marinara sauce (recipe page 106) or from a can

1 lb. brown mushrooms, sliced (optional)

3 cloves garlic, crushed and minced (optional)

1 cup water

1. Spray oil in the bottom of a 7-inch cake pan or ramekin. Place some noodles in the bottom (break them to size). Spoon on marinara sauce on top of the noodles. Sprinkle the meatball slices or if you use the sausage, pre-cook it with the mushrooms and garlic and sprinkle them on.

2. Scoop the ricotta cheese on top of the meat and finish the layer by covering it with mozzarella cheese. Follow this for a second layer. Finish the top with the remaining cheese.

3. Pour the water in the bottom of the Instant Pot®, place the trivet in the bottom, and set the lasagna on top of the trivet. Place the lid on the Instant Pot® and select manual, pressure, high for 30 minutes. Let the pot finish the cycle and bleed off naturally. Let it sit for 10 minutes or more before serving.

Beef Bourguignon

This is an easy recipe to make that will make a difference in your traditional Sunday dinner. It is super tasty served over mashed potatoes.

¼ cup canola oil

4-5 lbs. of beef chuck cut into 1-inch cubes, remove excess fat

Salt and pepper to taste

4 Tbsp. real butter

1 cup onions, ¼-inch diced

½ cup carrots, diced

½ cup celery, diced

5 Tbsp. flour

3 cups beef stock

3 Tbsp. tomato paste

1 Tbsp. beef base

Cornstarch and water mixed to a slurry (to thicken more after cooking if desired)

1. Set the Instant Pot® to sauté high. Add the oil and brown the beef well a few at a time and set aside. Season with sea salt and black pepper.

2. Melt the butter in the bottom and brown the onions, carrots, and celery. Be sure to scrape the bottom with a plastic or wooden scraper. Stir it well until it is browning. Stir in the flour mixing well. Cook for several minutes, whisking well until it smells like popcorn and starts to turn light brown.

3. Add the stock, tomato paste, and beef base. Stir it for a minute until is thickened. Cook for several minutes, strain out the veggies, and add the beef back to the pot. (You can discard the vegetables, or set them aside and add them back in at the end.) Stir the beef in well, place the lid on top, select meat/stew, and set the time for 40 minutes.

4. Let the pressure bleed off naturally. If it is not thick enough for your desire, add the cornstarch and water slurry a little at a time with the sauce boiling using the sauté function until it is to the thickness you want. Serve over potatoes or rice.

Chicken Gnocchi Soup

This recipe originated in Italy but has become famous here mainly because of Olive Garden. In my opinion, you can't beat the homemade version.

½ cup real butter

2 cups carrots, sliced

2 cups celery, sliced

3 cloves garlic, minced

6 Tbsp. flour

4 cups chicken stock

1 medium onion, diced ¼-inch

3 lbs. pulled and chopped rotisserie chicken or leftover turkey

3 bay leaves

1 tsp. white pepper

2 tsp. black pepper

1 (16-oz.) package large gnocchi potato pasta (found in the pasta aisle)

½ lb. baby spinach leaves, rinsed and drained

2 Tbsp. chicken base

2 cups heavy cream

1. Select sauté on the Instant Pot® and put the butter in the bottom and melt it. Add the onions, carrots, and celery, and cook until the onions are clear.

2. Add the minced garlic and stir in the flour. Stir it in well until the flour is well coated and saturated. Pour the chicken stock in and stir it well.

3. Add the chicken, bay leaves, pepper, Gnocchi pasta, spinach, and chicken base. Close the lid and select the soup function and set the time for 15 minutes. Let the pressure bleed off naturally.

4. Open the Instant Pot® and stir well taking special care to stir the bottom. Add the cream and slowly fold in before serving.

Wienerschnitzel

This traditional German dish is not associated with hot dogs in any way as the namesake fast food chain would suggest. Instead, it is a tender cooked beef with a mushroom brown sauce served over hand-cut noodles. Egg noodles can be used a as a substitute when time is a factor.

4 Tbsp. real butter

4 Tbsp. flour or cornstarch

2 cups water

2 Tbsp. Worcestershire sauce

1 Tbsp. beef base

4 cloves garlic, crushed (or 2 tsp. minced)

2 lbs. beef flank steak, chuck or London Broil, cut into large bite-sized chunks

1 lb. Crimini (brown) mushrooms kept whole

Salt and pepper to taste

1. Set the Instant Pot® to sauté, select the high option. Melt the butter in the bottom and whisk in the flour mixing well. Cook for several minutes whisking well until it smells like popcorn and starts to turn dark blonde.

2. Add the water, Worcestershire sauce, and beef base. Whisk it for a minute until is thickened. Add the garlic, beef chunks, and mushrooms.

3. Hit clear on the Instant Pot®. Place the lid on and turn the vent to pressure. Select the meat/stew switch and select high pressure. Let the Instant Pot® finish its cycle and let it bleed off naturally. Vent any remaining pressure and open the lid. Add salt and pepper to taste. Serve over egg noodles garnished with cheese.

Apple Braised Pork

This Italian dish is great served with roasted potatoes. It is very sweet and tender.

4 lbs. boneless pork shoulder or country-style spare ribs, cut into large chunks

3 tsp. sea salt

3 tsp. coarse ground black pepper

Flour to dredge

¼ cup canola oil

1 cup apple cider

1 tart apple, cored and sliced in half

1 medium sweet onion, kept whole with paper left on

4 cloves garlic, peeled and kept whole

1. Begin by seasoning the pork with the salt and pepper and dredging it through the flour enough to coat it well.

2. Heat up the canola oil in the bottom of the Instant Pot® by selecting sauté high. Brown the pork well a couple of pieces at a time if needed and set them aside.

3. Add the apple cider to the pot. Scrape the bottom with a plastic or wooden scraper making sure to scrape up all the chunks from the bottom. Add the pork to the bottom. Place the apple, onion, and garlic on the top.

4. Place the lid on the pot and set to manual pressure high. Set the time for 60 minutes. Let the pressure bleed off naturally. Remove the apple, onion, and garlic. Remove the pork and stir the sauce very well with a whisk. Serve by drizzling the sauce over the top of the pork.

Swiss Steaks

We ate this a lot when I was a kid. This version of it is very rich using the Sauce Tomate as the base.

1 lb. salt pork, pancetta, or bacon, diced

5 lbs. beef chuck, cut into cubes

2 cups sweet onions, ¼-inch diced

1 cup celery, diced

1 cup carrots, diced

2 cloves garlic, minced

2 cups tomatoes, diced

3 bay leaves

¼ cup fresh parsley

2 tsp. sea salt

2 tsp. coarse ground black pepper

1 tsp. thyme or 1 sprig of fresh thyme

3 cups chicken stock

1 Tbsp. beef base

1. Begin by selecting sauté on the Instant Pot®. Brown the salt pork, pancetta, or bacon really well. Remove the meat, leaving the grease behind.

2. Brown the beef a few pieces at a time and set them aside with the bacon. Add the onions, celery, and carrots to the grease. Stir well and cook until they are starting to brown.

3. Add the remaining ingredients. Place the lid on the pot, and select soup and set the time for 20 minutes. Let the pressure bleed off naturally.

4. Remove the bay leaves and blend the remainder of the ingredients until smooth using an immersion blender. Return the beef and bacon to the sauce, stir in well, close the lid, and select meat/stew. Set the time for 40 minutes. Let the pressure bleed off naturally. Serve over broiled potatoes.

Coq au Vin

This French chicken dish is amazing. Use a full chicken parted out to make it.

1 lb. salt pork, pancetta, or bacon, diced

Small roasting hen cut into pieces, skin kept on

2 cups sweet onions, ¼-inch diced

1 cup celery, diced

1 cup carrots, diced

1 tsp. sea salt (for seasoning the chicken)

1 tsp. black pepper (for seasoning the chicken)

3 Tbsp. real butter

3 Tbsp. flour

4 cloves garlic, minced

½ cup dry red wine, cooking wine, or cranberry juice

3 bay leaves

¼ cup of fresh parsley

2 tsp. sea salt

2 tsp. coarse ground black pepper

1 tsp. thyme or 1 sprig of fresh thyme

2 cups chicken stock

1. Begin by selecting sauté on the Instant Pot®. Brown the salt pork, pancetta, or bacon really well. Remove the meat leaving the grease behind. Brown the chicken one piece at a time and set them aside with the bacon.

2. Add the onions, celery, and carrots to the grease, stir well and cook until they are starting to brown.

3. Add the remaining ingredients, place the lid on the pot, and select soup and set the time for 20 minutes. Let the pressure bleed off naturally.

4. Remove the bay leaves and blend the remainder of the ingredients until smooth using an immersion blender.

5. Return the chicken and bacon to the sauce, stir in well, close the lid, and select meat/stew. Set the time for 25 minutes. Let the pressure bleed off naturally. Make sure the chicken is cooked to at least 165 degrees. Serve the pieces with the sauce drizzled over the top.

Chicken Picatta

This is one of those very quick easy meals that I really enjoy. You can serve it with pasta or rice or just have it as a stand-alone dish.

3 Tbsp. olive oil

2 tsp. sea salt

2 tsp. coarse ground black pepper

4 boneless skinless chicken breasts, fat removed

Flour for dredging

2 Tbsp. real butter

2 Tbsp. flour

1 cup chicken stock

¼ cup drained capers

1 lemon, zested and squeezed

2 cloves garlic, sliced

Fresh Italian Parsley chopped to garnish

Fresh shredded parmesan cheese to garnish

1. Pour the olive oil in the bottom of the Instant Pot®, select sauté and wait for the oil to get hot. Season the chicken breasts with the salt and pepper and dredge through the flour enough to coat. Brown the chicken on both sides and remove from the pot.

2. Add the butter and flour to the pot and whisk well, making sure to scrape the bottom. Continue whisking until the flour smells like popcorn. Slowly pour in the stock stirring well.

3. Add the capers, lemon juice, garlic, and lemon zest. Return the chicken to the pot and arrange as best as you can. Place the lid on the pot and select manual pressure high and set the time for 5 minutes. Bleed off the pressure manually and open the lid. Serve the chicken drizzled with the sauce and sprinkle the parsley and parmesan cheese over the top as a garnish.

CHICKEN ALFREDO | PAGE 106

BEEF STROGANOFF | PAGE 105

CHAPTER 8:
Pasta Recipes

I know a lot of people may think that pasta would fit into the Italian section, but these recipes are not Italian at all and I wouldn't want to mislead anyone in that regard. These are easy to make comfort food pasta recipes. The pressure cooker does well with them.

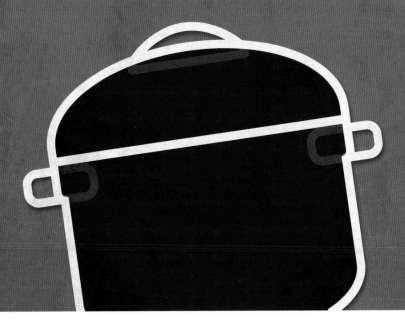

Beef Stroganoff

This is a family favorite recipe. I especially love a real honest-to-goodness from-scratch stroganoff. Serve over egg noodles or rice.

3 Tbsp. canola oil

3 lbs. beef chuck steaks, cut into small bite-sized pieces

2 lbs. brown mushrooms, sliced

4 cloves garlic, minced

1 stick real butter

6 Tbsp. flour

4 cups whole milk

2 tsp. sea salt

2 tsp. coarse ground black pepper

2 tsp. Worcestershire sauce

1 pint heavy cream

½ cup parmesan cheese, grated

1. Pour the oil into the bottom of the Instant Pot®. Set the Instant Pot® to sauté high and when the oil is hot, add the beef, mushrooms, and garlic, and brown well.

2. Add the butter and flour and stir well until incorporated. Add the remaining ingredients except the cream and the cheese.

3. Place the lid on and set the pot to meat/stew high and set the time for 40 minutes. Bleed off the pressure manually. Open the lid and stir in the cream and parmesan cheese a little at a time. Serve over rice or egg noodles.

Chicken Alfredo

This recipe from scratch is so much better than the stuff in a can. It will make it hard to ever go back especially for how easy it is to make. Serve over ziti noodles.

3 Tbsp. olive oil

6 cloves garlic, whole and peeled

2 lbs. chicken breast, diced

4 Tbsp. flour

4 Tbsp. real butter

4 cups whole milk

2 tsp. coarse ground black pepper

2 tsp. sea salt

1 pint heavy cream

8 oz. parmesan cheese, shredded

1 lb. cooked ziti noodles (optional for 1 pot)

1. Pour the oil into the Instant Pot® and set it to sauté high. Place the cloves of garlic whole and peeled into the olive oil and cook until they are browned. Remove the garlic from the Instant Pot® and set aside. When the garlic has cooled down, mince it.

2. Brown the chicken and remove. Mince the garlic. Add the flour and butter to the bottom and whisk well until the flour smells like popcorn.

3. Pour in the milk and add the pepper and sea salt. Add the garlic and the chicken. Place the lid on and set the pot to manual pressure high and set the time for 10 minutes. Bleed the pressure off manually.

4. Fold in the cream and add the parmesan cheese a little at a time stirring well until it is incorporated. Serve over the noodles or stir them in for a "casserole" style.

Chicken Bacon Ranch

This recipe is a solid great tasting easy recipe to make.

3 Tbsp. olive oil

1 lb. of bacon, cut into small pieces

2 lbs. chicken breast, diced

4 Tbsp. flour

4 Tbsp. real butter

6 cups whole milk

2 tsp. coarse ground black pepper

2 tsp. sea salt

1 lb. elbow macaroni noodles

1 packet Hidden Valley Ranch
  dressing mix

1 pint heavy cream

8 oz. Colby Jack cheese, shredded

1. Pour the oil into the Instant Pot® and set it to sauté high. Put the bacon in and cook it until crispy. Remove the bacon from the Instant Pot® and set aside.

2. Brown the chicken and remove. Add the flour and butter to the bottom and whisk well until the flour smells like popcorn. Pour in the milk and add the pepper, ranch packet, sea salt, macaroni, and the chicken. Place the lid on and set the pot to manual pressure high and set the time for 10 minutes. Bleed the pressure off manually.

3. Fold in the cream and add the cheese a little at a time stirring well until it is incorporated. Stir the bacon bits back in before serving.

Cheesy Chicken Ziti

This is a very tasty comfort food type of dish. You can use leftover rotisserie chicken or leftover turkey if you don't want to use fresh chicken to make this.

3 Tbsp. olive oil

4 boneless skinless chicken breasts, diced

2 cloves garlic, peeled and kept whole

4 Tbsp. real butter

4 Tbsp. flour

6 cups whole milk

2 tsp. sea salt

1 tsp. black pepper

1 tsp. white pepper

1 lb. dried ziti noodles

1 lb. broccoli florets, cut bite-size and rinsed

½ pint heavy cream

8 oz. American cheese, cut into chunks (buy at your local deli)

8 oz. cheddar cheese, shredded

1. Begin by pouring the olive oil in the bottom of the Instant Pot®. Select sauté high and wait for the pan to get hot. Add the garlic and cook until you can smell it well. Add the chicken and vigorously stir and cook until it is beginning to look mostly white.

2. Add the butter and the flour and stir well until both are well incorporated into the chicken. Continue stirring while you add the milk, salt, pepper, ziti noodles, and broccoli. Place the lid on the Instant Pot® and select manual pressure medium and set the timer for 5 minutes. Bleed off the pressure manually and open the lid. Stir the contents together well and slowly fold in the cream, American cheese, and cheddar cheese. Let it stand for 5 minutes before serving.

Cordon Bleu Pasta

I'm not sure how this combination came together, but it's something we've been cooking for a while in my family and everyone seems to like it pretty well. Serve it over rice or noodles.

2 Tbsp. olive oil

2 lbs. chicken breast, diced

1 lb. sweet slice ham, cut into strips

4 cloves garlic, minced

1 (14-oz.) can diced tomatoes, drained

1 cup ricotta cheese

½ pint cream

1 lemon, squeezed

6 fresh basil leaves, hand shredded

1 lb. penne pasta

2 tsp. black pepper

2 tsp. sea salt

½ lb. mozzarella cheese, shredded

½ lb. swiss cheese, shredded

1. Add the olive oil to the Instant Pot®, select sauté high and brown the chicken with the ham and the garlic.

2. Add the remaining ingredients, except the cheeses. Place the lid on and select manual pressure and set the time for 15 minutes. Bleed the pressure off manually.

3. Remove the lid, stir well, and cover the top with the mozzarella and swiss cheese. Put the lid back on and let it sit for 10 minutes before serving.

PEACH COBBLER | PAGE 120

STRAWBERRY RHUBARB CRUMBLE | PAGE 117

PUMPKIN CAKE | PAGE 118

CHAPTER 9:
Desserts

I would have never considered cooking a dessert in a pressure cooker before the Instant Pot® came along. I've seen recipes online so I thought, why not? It's an interesting process and definitely different than baking. The results turned out great though, so, why not?

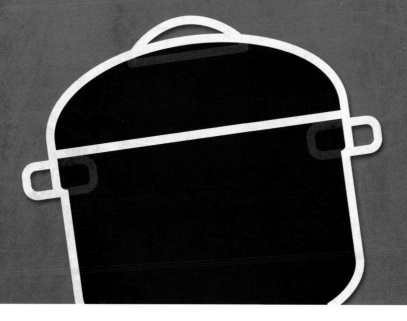

Strawberry Shortcake

This recipe was very surprising to me. I could not believe how well the shortcake turned out. It was a different texture to be sure, but moist and nice.

5 cups fresh strawberries, sliced

1½ cups sugar

2 cups white flour

¼ cup white sugar

4 tsp. baking powder

½ tsp. salt

1 stick real butter

1 egg

½ cup milk

1 cup water

Heavy cream to drizzle over the top or be whipped for a topping

1. Cut the strawberries and mix them in a bowl with the sugar and let them sit for at least an hour to macerate.

2. In a mixing bowl, mix the flour, sugar, baking powder, and salt. Cut the butter into the flour mixture until it is coarse lumps.

3. Mix the egg and milk together and fold it into the shortcake mixture. Using individual size baking dishes that are greased, and fill the dishes with the shortcake mixture.

4. In the Instant Pot®, add the water and place the trivet in the bottom. Place the shortcake dish on top of the trivet and close the lid. Set the Instant Pot® to manual pressure high, and cook for 7 minutes. Bleed off the pressure manually and cook the remaining shortcakes in like manner.

5. Let them stand for a few minutes before serving. To serve, drizzle the strawberries over the shortcakes and the cream.

German Chocolate Cake

This sounded so crazy to me at first, cake in a pressure cooker! I was skeptical until I tried it. I am a believer now. It is so moist and nice in texture.

2 cups flour	3 eggs
2 cups sugar	½ cup real butter melted
1½ tsp. baking soda	1 cup milk
1½ tsp. baking powder	1 tsp. vanilla
2 tsp. salt	1 cup boiling water
¾ cup of Hershey's Special Dark Cocoa	1 can caramel pecan frosting

1. Mix all of the dry ingredients together in a bowl. Add all the wet ingredients except the water. Mix it well for several minutes. Slowly stir in the boiling water. Pour the batter into a greased 7-inch round cake pan (it will take 2 pans full for this recipe).

2. Place 1 cup of water in the bottom of the Instant Pot®. Set the trivet in the bottom. Make a sling with foil folded into strips and lower the cake pan into the Instant Pot®. Place the lid on and set the Instant Pot® to manual pressure and high for 15 minutes.

3. Let the Instant Pot® bleed off naturally for an additional 10 minutes. Bleed off the remaining pressure manually and remove the cake from the pot. Follow this for the next cake. Let it stand for 30 minutes before frosting and serving.

Crème Brûlée

This classic French dessert can be made simple in the Instant Pot®. The control temperatures make it very easy to achieve the desired results.

1 pint heavy cream

3 egg yolks, beaten

⅓ cup sugar

1 tsp. vanilla

1 cup water

1. In a saucepan on the stove, heat the cream to the scalded state (where it's just starting to bubble around the edges).

2. While the cream is getting warm, mix the egg yolks, sugar, and vanilla thoroughly. Whisk the cream into the eggs one spoonful at a time until fully incorporated. This will temper the eggs.

3. Place one cup of water into the Instant Pot® and set the trivet inside. Turn the Instant Pot® on sauté until the water starts to boil. Pour the brûlée mixture into ramekins and set carefully onto the trivet. You will probably have to do these individually, depending on the size of your ramekin.

4. Place the lid on, turn the Instant Pot® to manual pressure low, and cook for ten minutes. Bleed off manually, and remove the ramekin. Do this until all are cooked.

5. Chill the crème brûlées in the fridge for several hours. Before serving, sprinkle granulated sugar on top. Using a propane or butane torch, brûlée the sugar until caramelized on top. Serve. Note: It's important to coat the entire surface of the crème brûlée or you may burn the custard.

Strawberry Rhubarb Crumble

Strawberry rhubarb is one of my favorite flavor combinations for dessert. It won't get as crispy as doing it in the oven, but it cooks a whole lot faster.

FOR THE FILLING

3 cups fresh strawberries (or frozen if out of season), sliced

2 cups rhubarb, sliced

1½ cups sugar

½ cup flour

½ cup water

FOR THE CRUMBLE

1 cup butter, softened

2 cups flour

1 cup brown sugar

1 tsp. salt

1. Mix the strawberries, rhubarb, sugar, and flour together in a bowl. Stir until all the flour is incorporated. Let it stand.

2. In a separate bowl, mix the crumble ingredients together until well incorporated.

3. Set the Instant Pot® to sauté and add the water. Let it heat until boiling. Add the strawberry and rhubarb mixture on top of the water. In your hand, take a handful of the crumble, squeeze it together until packed, and crumble it with your fingers over the top of the strawberry mixture.

4. Close the lid, cook on manual high pressure for 25 minutes. Let it bleed off naturally, open the lid, and let it stand for fifteen minutes. Serve with vanilla ice cream.

Pumpkin Cake

This is one of my favorite cake recipes. We have won many awards for this recipe. Frost this cake with a cream cheese frosting.

¾ cup flour

½ tsp. baking powder

½ tsp. baking soda

½ tsp. cinnamon

½ tsp. ground cloves

¼ tsp. salt

3 large eggs

1 cup white sugar

⅔ cup 100% pure pumpkin puree

1. Mix all the ingredients together thoroughly, and pour into a well-greased ramekin or 7-inch cake pan.

2. Pour one cup of water into the bottom of the Instant Pot®, place the trivet in the bottom, set the ramekins or cake pan on the trivet. Close the lid, select manual pressure high, and set the time for ten minutes.

3. Bleed the pressure off manually, and repeat the cycle with the rest of the batter. Frost with cream cheese frosting when it's cooled down.

Lemon Poppy Seed Cake

Few desserts beat a glazed lemon poppy seed cake. You can do these in individual ramekins, or a larger 7-inch cake.

CAKE

3 Tbsp. poppy seeds

¾ cups buttermilk

¼ cup milk

4 eggs

1 cup butter, softened

1¾ cup white sugar

3 cups flour

1 tsp. vanilla

2 lemons, zested and squeezed

1 tsp. baking soda

1 tsp. baking powder

GLAZE

1½ cups powdered sugar

1 Tbsp. butter

2 Tbsp. lemon juice

1. Two hours before, mix the poppy seeds, buttermilk, and milk. Let them sit.

2. When you are ready to bake, mix 3 eggs, butter, and sugar until very fluffy. Add the remaining cake ingredients and mix well. Pour into well-greased ramekins or 7-inch cake pan.

3. Pour 1 cup of water in the bottom of the Instant Pot®, select manual pressure high, and 15 minutes. When the cycle is done, relieve the pressure manually, then follow this procedure until the rest is cooked.

4. Let the cake cool for twenty minutes before glazing. Mix the ingredients together of the glaze, then spread over the cake while it is still warm.

Peach Cobbler

This is definitely not the same dump cake cobbler that so many people are familiar with. This is much more authentic and flavorful. In Utah, we have amazing fresh-grown peaches that taste so good in this recipe.

FOR THE PEACHES

6-10 fresh peaches, sliced, or 6
    cups canned peaches, drained

1½ cups white sugar

2 Tbsp. flour

2 Tbsp. corn starch

1 tsp. lemon juice

FOR THE TOPPING

2 cups flour

¾ cup sugar

1½ tsp. baking powder

1 tsp. salt

8 Tbsp. butter

1 cup buttermilk

1. Combine all the ingredients for the peaches. Pour ½ cup water in the bottom of the Instant Pot®, turn it on to sauté, and boil the water. Add the peaches and let it cook.

2. In the meantime, for the topping, mix the flour, sugar, baking powder, and salt together. Cut in the butter with a pastry cutter until pea size. Stir in the buttermilk.

3. Drop spoonfuls of the topping onto the peach mixture, close the lid, select manual pressure high and set the time for 20 minutes. Let it bleed off naturally and serve. Best served with vanilla ice cream.

Mixed Berry Cobbler

This recipe is one of my most requested recipes. I love the mix of tart berries and the sweet cobbler.

FOR THE BERRIES

6 cups of fresh or frozen mixed berries

1½ cups white sugar

2 Tbsp. flour

2 Tbsp. cornstarch

1 tsp. lemon juice

FOR THE TOPPING

2 cups flour

¾ cup sugar

1½ tsp. baking powder

1 tsp. salt

8 Tbsp. butter

1 cup buttermilk

1. Combine all the ingredients for the berries.

2. Pour ½ cup water in the bottom of the Instant Pot®, turn it on to sauté, and boil the water. Add the berries and let it cook.

3. In the meantime, for the topping, mix the flour, sugar, baking powder, and salt together. Cut in the butter with a pastry cutter until pea size. Stir in the buttermilk.

4. Drop spoonfuls of the topping onto the berry mixture, close the lid, select manual pressure high and set the time for 20 minutes. Let it bleed off naturally and serve. Best served with vanilla ice cream.

Index

About the Author

MATT PELTON grew up in Central Utah where he found his love for cooking in the outdoors. He learned to cook in a dutch oven at the age of eight and has done it ever since. He brought a 10-inch dutch oven with him on his LDS mission to Boston where he expanded his cooking abilities, learning to cook foods from all different cultures around the world. Matt started competing in pro division dutch oven and BBQ circuit. He has won two world championships from The International Dutch Oven Society in 2012 and 2013. He has also won many awards for his BBQ cooking, especially in the brisket category. Matt has also competed in the invitational World Food Championships aired on TV twice where he placed 3rd and 11th place respectively. Matt has appeared on TV numerous times for cooking most recently on the Travel Channel's "BBQ Crawl season 3." Matt has also worked as a chef at Deer Valley ski resorts in Utah often working with the other chefs there on proteins. Matt lives in Provo, Utah, with his wife, Katie, and three kids: Megan, Tristan, and Braxton. Matt enjoys mountain biking, hiking, hunting, fishing, and doing pretty much anything outdoors.